the
creative art
of
needlepoint
tapestry

Joan Fisher

Hamlyn
London · New York · Sydney · Toronto

Consultant editor
Marjorie Halligan

The author gratefully acknowledges the help and
co-operation given by Mr. J. Clark, of J. & P. Coats,
Glasgow, and Mr. R. C. Yates, of Wm. Briggs, Bolton, in
the preparation of this book.

Published by The Hamlyn Publishing Group Limited
London — New York — Sydney — Toronto
Hamlyn House, Feltham, Middlesex, England

Printed by The Senefelder Printing Co. Ltd, Purmerend

contents

introduction

First, a word of explanation about the subject matter of this book. The branch of creative needlecraft with which we are concerned is known variously—and confusingly—by a number of different names: needlepoint, needlework tapestry, tapestry work, canvas work, canvas embroidery . . . All these terms can be used, with accuracy, to describe the particular form of embroidery we deal with in this book. Which term you yourself use will depend on where you live, your background, how you came to be introduced to the craft, and other such factors.

Needlepoint is really a misnomer as no needle points are ever used in the work. And to some people needlework tapestry means embroidery on canvas worked entirely in tent stitch, as this produces an effect closely resembling woven tapestry. But to work only in tent stitch can be tedious indeed—not only to execute, but in the finished result too. This book offers a guide to *all* embroidery done on a canvas ground—this, of course, includes tent stitch but it encompasses many more decorative stitches too. After all, if you have a piece of canvas in front of you, and a needle and thread in your hand, why limit yourself to one stitch only?

There is a vast and very exciting range of stitches available which can be effectively worked on canvas—many of these stitches, traditional and modern varieties, you will find in the comprehensive dictionary of stiches beginning on page 42. And this need not be the limit to your stitch vocabulary. Once you have acquired a working knowledge of threads and canvas, you will go on to make up your own stitches—for this is what canvas embroidery is all about. Also, by using a variety of stitches you will achieve an interesting texture which in some ways has more appeal than the flatness of woven tapestry.

The form and outline of a canvas stitch is always dependent on the framework of the canvas itself. But despite the apparent restrictions of always working on a geometric grid—which is in fact what canvas imposes—wonderfully intricate and varied work can be done, from big-scale hangings stitched with thick threads on wide-mesh rug canvas, to beautifully fine and delicate canvas 'paintings' worked with silks on close-meshed canvas.

The canvas, the threads, the stitches themselves can all be made to play their part in creating individual designs to reflect your own personality, tastes and even your way of life. This is not a difficult art, and it is an immensely satisfying one. Even if you have never tried any form of embroidery before, work just a few simple stitches on a piece of wide-mesh canvas—and you should instantly discover the fascination of the age-old craft of canvas embroidery . . . tapestry needlework . . . Call it what you will! It's the craft itself that matters.

JOAN FISHER

how it all began

When man first invented clothes, he had to find a method of fashioning his garments, of putting them together, and of repairing them when they were torn, and so a 'needle' was devised—of thorn, fishbone, or whatever natural and suitable material was available. For 'thread', animal and plant fibres were used. Soon it was found that stitches could be decorative as well as functional, and embroidery was born. The stitching may have been crude, the materials primitive, but nevertheless this was the beginning of the art of embroidery.

It was not long before two distinct styles of embroidery evolved: one a free-style of decorative stitching on any type of material; the other a geometric technique based on following, as it is natural to do, the mesh of a coarse linen, net or open web. This type of embroidery on an evenweave fabric where design is founded on the counting of threads has been used since earliest history. The stitches and patterns our ancestors formed in relation to the threads of the fabric were the precursors of the canvas stitches and patterns we know today.

A stitch inevitably bears some relation to the material on which it is worked, but canvas or a coarse linen almost compels a stitch based upon the cross lines of its weft. Evidence of this rigid construction of stitches and design can be seen in ancient Byzantine and Coptic embroidery, in Cretan work, and in peasant embroidery the world over.

An example of 17th century peasant embroidery, from the Greek islands. A cross stitch design of conventional flowers and birds is worked in coloured silks on a linen ground.

5

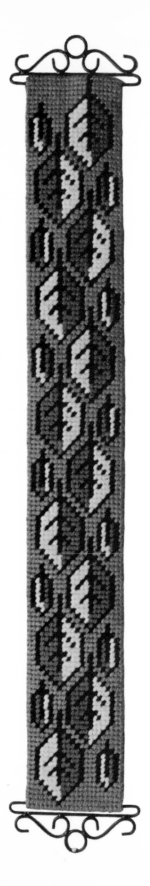

Most cultures of the ancient and modern world have evolved their own style of counted thread work as well as free style embroidery: the colourful Florentine work of 17th-century Italy and Hungary; the knotted carpets of Turkey; the boldly vibrant Norweave designs from Scandinavia; the beautiful satin stitch embroidery of the Persians, worked in white silk upon fine evenweave linen. Cross stitch, in particular, is probably the earliest counted thread stitch group of all, and has been developed into many different national styles throughout Europe, North Africa, and the Middle East. In more recent times, in the Victorian era, cross stitch formed the basis for Berlin woolwork which was so immensely popular with needle-women on both sides of the Atlantic.

Although canvas itself is an ancient material—its name comes from *cannabis* meaning hemp—it was not widely used as a ground for embroidery until Tudor times. Nevertheless, there is evidence to show that the art of embroidering on canvas—or a material very similar to canvas—was known in Roman times, and the late Anglo-Saxons were also skilled embroiderers.

The oldest surviving pieces of tapestry embroidery are in fragments. When the tomb of Archbishop Hubert Walter in Canterbury Cathedral, England, was opened in the 19th century, a ribbon stole was found among the relics. It has been dated at around 1200, although it could be older. Both the pattern and ground are worked in plait stitch.

The original foundation material has perished completely and the embroidery exists only because the stitches hold it together. But it can still be seen that the vanished material was similar to the embroidery canvas used today. The silk thread makes a geometric pattern of crucifixes and other shapes in brown, green and amber and, because of its simplicity, it has a strangely modern look.

Opus anglicanum
The first great and splendid period of English embroidery began in the 13th century and is known as the Opus anglicanum. Most of the work was on church vestments, though embroidery in the style of Opus anglicanum, rich with gold backgrounds and luxurious stitchery, was also in great demand by royalty and nobility (the only people who could afford it) throughout Europe. Although there are few examples of canvas embroidery in Opus anglicanum work, one of the finest and most famous examples surviving—the Syon Cope—is edged with rich tapestry embroidery.

The Cope is a great semi-circular cloak. The body is embroidered with gilt and silver thread and coloured silks, showing religious scenes. The original brilliant red of the ground colour has faded to a pleasing rusty brown, whilst the complementary green has held its colour rather better. But the tapestry embroidered borders—in cross stitch and long-armed cross stitch—have held their colours well. The pattern is of shields and other heraldic emblems, using silk in a very fine stitch.

The Syon Cope is so named because it belonged for a long time to the Bridgettine nuns at their convent at Syon, Isleworth, near London. Henry V founded the convent in 1414—15 and the cope went there shortly afterwards. The Bridgettine nuns

left England during the reign of Queen Elizabeth I, taking the cope with them. They kept it whilst wandering through Flanders, down through France and finally to Lisbon in Portugal. Eventually they returned to England in 1830, with the cope. It then went into private ownership before passing to the Victoria and Albert Museum, London, in 1864, where it can be seen today.

A 13th-century English orphrey (a panel separately made and stitched to the back of a cope or chasuble) at Lyons includes panels of tent stitch in its design. Many other examples exist—a cape at Pienza and an orphrey featuring chequer stitch at Lerida, in northern Spain.

English embroidery during this Opus anglicanum period was so prized that an inventory taken at the Vatican in 1295 contained more of the precious English embroidery than of any other kind. Because of the great amounts of gold and silver thread used in the work, along with seed pearls and semi-precious stones, Opus anglicanum had a high cost as well as being treasured for the quality and artistic beauty of the embroidery. London merchants found it was a good investment to finance the making of these vestments. Professional embroiderers, mostly in London, were engaged to do the actual sewing—but only after an apprenticeship lasting seven hard years.

The Tudor era
With the coming of the Plague and with Europe unsettled by constant wars, Opus anglicanum faded out towards the end of the 14th century. Although much embroidery was still done for the church, it became stereotyped and of poorer quality. In the second half of the 15th century Flanders became the new leader in western European embroidery.

The coming of the Tudor monarchy in England led to settled times and another great period of English embroidery which influenced the rest of Europe. Embroidery on canvas began to be widely practised, and it gained a popularity it has never lost. A

An example of stumpwork on white satin, with draperies of twisted coloured silks worked over canvas, and of needlepoint lace-stitched gimp. The panel is believed to show Charles I under a tent with Queen Henrietta Maria, with a lady in attendance on one side and a chamberlain on the other.

knotted kind of stitching on canvas, imitating Turkish carpets and known as Turkey work, came into use for chair and stool cushions.

By the time Elizabeth I was on the throne (1558—1603), domestic embroidery—both by private needlewomen and professionals—was a popular pastime. Everything possible was richly embroidered, and a wide variety of styles was used.

In a private collection in England is a canvas embroidered cushion cover which is supposed to be the work of Queen Elizabeth I herself. It shows a low bowl containing a great, graceful spray of flowers. The stitching is rather uneven, the shading simple and the back of the work is not finished off as neatly as it could be. But the overall attractiveness more than makes up for its faults and it is a fascinating memento from a great woman.

Mary Queen of Scots, Elizabeth's famous prisoner, was guarded from 1569 to 1584 by George Talbot, sixth Earl of Shrewsbury and fourth husband to Bess of Hardwick. Both Mary and Bess were famous neeedlewomen and during the first four or five years of Mary's imprisonment at Hardwick the two women worked together on several large projects which survive to this day.

Bess's husband wrote, in a letter in 1569: 'This Queen continueth daily to resort unto my wife's chamber where she useth to sit working with the needle in which she much delighteth and in devising works'

The most famous of these joint works is a set of four wall hangings, one of which is dated 1570. Known as the Oxburgh Hangings, they are of green velvet decorated lavishly with panels embroidered on linen canvas. The work is done in coloured silks and silver-gilt thread in cross, tent and long-armed cross stitches.

These hangings effectively illustrate several facets of Elizabethan amateur embroidery. Emblems and devices to record events in their own lives were a favourite inclusion in the Elizabethans' embroidery. One of the main panels on Mary and Bess's work shows a ball-shaped cage surrounded by a spray of falling feathers with the motto: 'Sorrows pass but hope abides'.

The border contains the arms of England, Scotland, Spain and France along with emblems copied from *Devises Heroiques*, a book published in France in 1557. The remaining spaces on the square panel are filled with a maritime scene. The waters are positively boiling with creatures of the sea—a very fishy serpent, a scaled and finned beast with the head and tusks of a boar, a sea horse with curly mermaid tail and hooved forelegs, and a frilly octopus. A rather astonished duck sits in a corner surveying this menagerie which is both charmingly naive and fascinatingly attractive.

When not drawing upon their own imaginations for the fabulous creatures they loved to portray, the Elizabethans turned to books, such as the one mentioned above, for their illustrations. The Oxburgh panels include several animals which were doubtless taken from drawings in *History of Animals* by Conrad Gesner, first published in Zurich in 1560. Two very obvious copies are of an elephant and a highly unreal ape. In both cases the embroidered copy is much more attractive than the original drawing and the elephant, in particular, looks much more authentic in the embroidery.

These smaller panels are of a higher standard of draughtsmanship than the main panel. A particularly attractive one, showing a flowering plant, bears Bess of Hardwick's monogram (ES) and another uplifting motto: 'True courage seeks danger'

One of the four hangings has been cut up to make a bed valance. This is now in the collection of the Victoria and Albert Museum, London. The three intact hangings are at Oxburgh Hall, Norfolk.

Large and reasonably affluent households where a great deal of embroidery was done—such as Bess of Hardwick's—normally employed a professional embroiderer. Apart from undertaking some of the actual stitching, the professional would also be a draughtsman who could adapt book illustrations for canvas and free-style embroidery work. In fact any pattern desired by the embroideress would be designed and drawn on the canvas for her by her professional embroiderer, ready for her to do the actual stitching. It would seem that the animal drawings taken from Gesner's book for Mary and Bess's work were adapted for them by someone with a good eye for line and design.

Embroidery was also frequently a communal occupation. Bess of Hardwick is known to have encouraged her maids, pages and even grooms to help her with the work. There exists correspondence between Bess and her husband, Lord Shrewsbury, which

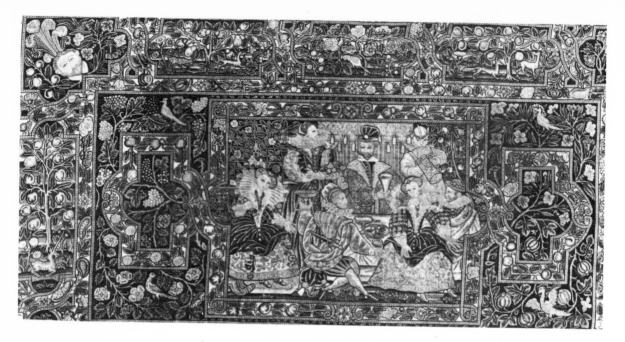

Lucretia's Banquet, a carpet in linen canvas embroidered with wool and silk in tent stitch; late 16th century.

concerns an argument over ownership of certain embroideries at a time when the couple had fallen out. Bess claimed that the work had been done by her own personal servants, not her husband's, and therefore the disputed embroideries should remain in her possession. And apparently they did.

First pattern books

At this time there appeared books of patterns designed for the embroideress's benefit. *La Clef des Champs*, by Jacques Le Moyne De Morgue, published in 1586 in London, was one of these early pattern books.

Elizabethans delighted in gardens, particularly herb gardens. They were keenly interested in horticulture and this is reflected in the illustrated literature of the time. But nowhere is their joy in natural beauties more apparent than in their embroidery. It abounds with flowers and fruit, animals and trees. Favourite flowers were the rose, honeysuckle, foxglove, iris, daffodil, carnation, pink, columbine, primrose and violet.

These flowers, sometimes drawn extremely naturally, sometimes formally and sometimes most imaginatively, are nevertheless nearly always exuberantly gay. And all these treatments accorded well with canvas embroidery.

Almost everything in sight was decorated by the Elizabethans. Not many examples of their ornamented clothing have survived, for the embroidery on the great court costumes of the time was enhanced with pearls and precious or semi-precious stones and would be dismantled when the clothing was no longer wanted. Fortunately the canvas embroidery of the time was not so treated and because it is also more hardwearing, much of it has survived for our present enjoyment.

Armchairs in those days were a rarity and were usually reserved for the master and perhaps the mistress of the household. For the rest of the family and for visitors, there was a choice of benches, forms or window seats. Both for comfort and

Long cushion cover in linen canvas embroidered with silk in tent stitch; mid to late 16th century.

to enhance their sparsely furnished rooms, the Elizabethans supplied themselves with exquisitely decorated cushions. These were usually generous-sized squares or rectangles. Other shapes do not appear to have been used. Here canvas embroidery was widely employed, in tent and varieties of cross stitch, using silk or wool and occasionally metal threads.

One of the examples in the Victoria and Albert Museum's great embroidery collection is a rectangular cushion cover embroidered with many-coloured silks in tent stitch, made in the mid-16th century. The centre shows the coat of arms of John Warneford and his wife Susanna Yates of Sevenhampton, Wiltshire. Surrounding this is an exuberance of flowers and bright dragonflies, with a charming pair of big-eyed frogs nestling under great, curling leaves. All this is bordered by a chain of honeysuckle blossoms.

The work—not to mention the skill—which this one cushion cover demanded must have been phenomenal. It is not surprising, therefore, that needlewomen used assistant embroiderers whenever possible.

At the end of the Opus anglicanum period, when demand for vestments was still great, production was speeded up by embroidering decorative figures through fine linen on to a rich ground of velvet or silk. A similar method of completing a large, richly decorated item with less work was used by the Elizabethans but here—as in the case of the Oxburgh Hangings—the embroidery was generally worked on separate canvas panels and applied to the ground when finished.

Embroidery slips as well as panels were used. These were not simple squared or rounded shapes, but intricately indented forms of single items—usually flowers. This could be why they were called slips, because they resembled slips taken from plants for rooting or grafting.

The slips were embroidered on canvas—usually in silks—trimmed out and applied to a rich ground cloth such as velvet. A superb surviving example of this work is embroidered in silk, silver-gilt and silver threads using tent, cross, long-armed cross and stem stitches and laid work. The cut-out shapes of flowers, insects, birds and fabulous animals are so intricate that in this case the work would more easily have been done on one continuous piece of canvas. But the black velvet ground is the ideal foil for the rich colours and the piece is one of the most beautiful Elizabethan embroideries to be seen.

A good many slips of this kind are still in existence. Presumably the items they were intended to decorate were never finished but the beautifully worked slips have been preserved from generation to generation. In most cases the canvas is crammed full of slips, waiting to be trimmed out.

Another lovely example of slip work is a hanging or bed curtain, originally from Scone Castle, now to be seen at the Royal Scottish Museum, Edinburgh.

One reason given for the increased popularity of embroidery during this period was the new availability of metal needles. Elias Crowse, a German, is known to have been teaching the manufacture of Spanish needles in London in 1566. Up till then the bone needles used in Saxon times were possibly the only available tools.

Table carpets

Yet another factor leading to increased demand for tapestry needlework was the new fashion for handsome floor coverings, although rushes and other similar straws were the most common up to the end of the 16th century. One visitor to Queen Elizabeth in 1596 noticed with some surprise that her presence chamber was 'strewn with hay'.

Table carpets began to be worked: these were sometimes stitched in silk on canvas in tent stitch, sometimes in a mixture of silk and wool in long-armed cross stitch, and sometimes even in couched metal thread on velvet.

Cushion cover, dated 1604, showing the arms of the city of Hereford, England. Embroidery is worked in tent stitch with wool and some silk on a linen canvas ground.

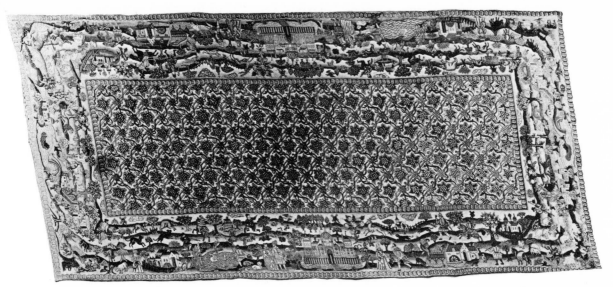

The attractive Gifford Table Carpet, made about 1550, is the earliest known English canvas embroidered carpet. In many-coloured wools, on linen canvas, the work is exceedingly fine, having twenty tent stitches to the inch. The main decoration is the Gifford arms, surrounded by a wreath of flowers. Incidentally, the floral wreath is so similar in style to the wreath on the long cushion cover mentioned above that both must have had the same inspiration—probably a pattern book.

The ground of the Gifford carpet, and the borders, are worked in a small, restrained, formal design. It does not mix very well with the larger-scale floral wreaths (there are three altogether), yet no doubt this did not bother the flower-loving Elizabethans in the least.

The most magnificent known piece of embroidery from the period is the Bradford Table Carpet, made in the late 16th century. This is again very fine work—twenty stitches to the inch—all in tent stitch with coloured silks. As often happens with tent stitching, the carpet has pulled badly out of shape on the diagonal. It is now shown hanging upright (Victoria and Albert Museum, London) but at one time it was displayed on a specially made irregular table so that the work could be clearly seen.

On the ground of the carpet is a repeated fruiting vine on trelliswork. The real beauty comes in the borders—about 15in deep. They show a country scene of great liveliness and charm. As in so much work of the period, very little attention is given to proportion or to perspective, so that the people are taller than the trees and yet the hazel nuts on one tree are larger than the people's heads!

There is so much of country life going on in the picture that it is almost impossible to describe, but in one space no more than 18in. long we are shown scenes of hunting, fishing and shooting along with two houses, two dogs and other similar domestic groups. At one point a naked man (perhaps a hermit?) is seen climbing into a tree. There are several such fascinating, unexplained cameos and one can only suppose that the carpet tells the history of a real, particular place.

The Bradford Table Carpet, a magnificent example of 16th century English work, embroidered in tent stitch with coloured silks, and depicting scenes of English country life.

An intricate embroidery in tent stitch, worked with silk and wool threads on canvas; early 17th century.

No less than twenty-three colours are used on the carpet, and although it must have faded since it was originally worked it is still beautifully coloured now.

The Bradford Table Carpet measures 13ft. by 5ft. 9in. This size, along with the minute stitching, high standard of work and intricacy of the pattern, points to the hand of a professional embroiderer—or embroiderers.

This type of scene was extremely popular at the time throughout Europe, where canvas embroidered table covers were in great demand. They were particularly popular in Holland and remained so—along with a preference for pastoral scenes—for a very long time.

Table carpets of this period, in tent or tent and cross stitch, were very often patterned to resemble the Turkish carpets which were beginning to come into fashion in Europe.

There is a table carpet at Hardwick, dated 1574, which shows the Judgement of Paris on a central medallion with borders of fruit, roses, birds and animals.

Wool and silk in tent stitch were often used together to superb effect, as in a beautiful carpet of the period which illustrates Lucretia's Banquet. Strapwork panels divide areas packed with fruiting vines, trees and bushes. The corner panels show four different heads, each sprouting great sprays of ostrich feathers.

The style of that carpet is rather more sophisticated than the usual English embroidery of the time. Mary Queen of Scots is credited with introducing this type of work to England, via Scotland. A good many bed valances of the period have survived, showing figures in clothing worn at the French court in the late 16th century. These are finely embroidered in silk and wool in tent stitch and sometimes include raised work. The stitching is so fine that the work often resembles a woven tapestry.

Scenes from the Old Testament or tales from Ovid's *Metamorphoses* were particular favourites for bed valances. These were almost invariably given riotous garden backgrounds. In one example, the story includes a man in a great four-poster bed, yet the house is indicated only by a few pillars and a tiled floor so that the action may spill out into gardens on either side.

Many bed valances still in existence must have been parts of complete sets of bed furnishings. But the accompanying bed hangings and spreads, which—judging by the valances—must have been magnificent, were subjected to greater wear and tear and are no longer in existence.

With their passion for decorating everything within sight, it is not surprising that the Elizabethans produced many exquisite handbags in canvas embroidery. The surviving examples were richly worked in coloured silks, silver-gilt and silver threads in chain, tent, gobelin and plaited braid stitches. They were further decorated with plaited drawstrings, cords and tassels of silk. Favourite designs were trees or coiled branches bearing large flowers and fruit. Padding was used to raise the flower petals, or sometimes the flowers were made separately and then partially fixed to the canvas. In this case the ground might be covered through with silver-gilt or silver embroidery.

In 1598 a certain Jane Bostocke stitched the oldest known sampler. Samplers were known before Elizabethan times, but none has come down to us. Jane's charming work is inscribed: 'Alice Lee was borne the 23 of November being Tuesday in the afternoone 1596'. Perhaps she meant it for a gift to the child, as a useful reference to the many complex patterns and stitches which follow the inscription. The stitches, in metal and silk threads, are on linen. A few pieces carrying experiments with design for cushions or table carpets on linen canvas also exist.

Most samplers were at that time intended for reference to the stitches illustrated on them and were not intended as show pieces, as were some later samplers.

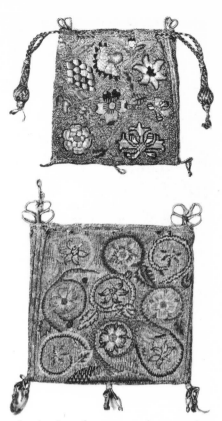

A selection of canvas work purses, late 16th and early 17th century. Top of page: tent and plaited braid stitches worked with silk, silver-gilt and silver threads. Above: tent and long-armed cross stitches worked with silk and silver-gilt threads. Far left: tent, gobelin and plaited braid stitches worked with silk and silver threads. Near left: chain and stem stitches with buttonholing, worked with silk and silver-gilt threads.

A panel from the Hatton Garden wall hangings.

Changing styles

During the first part of the 17th century embroidery continued to maintain its popularity. But gradually styles were changing.

Samplers began to be worked more extensively. The earliest examples are short and broad, worked in coloured silks and metal threads on loosely woven linen. Scattered motifs of birds, animals, trees, flowers and geometric patterns are used, with back, plaited braid, tent, cross, Algerian eye and other canvas stitches. Other samplers are long and narrow, sometimes signed and dated, worked in silk on soft linen, sometimes with whitework, cutwork and openwork.

One of the few large canvas embroideries coming from this period is a table covering measuring 10ft. 7in. by 7ft. 6in. It is in tent stitch with silk, wool and metal threads and is believed to celebrate the restoration of the monarchy when Charles II came to the throne. Its huge central panel shows Justice, with eyes uncovered, being given a heavenly crown of wisdom by an angel reaching down from a cloud. The carpet is scattered with fruits and flowers, and other allegorical figures.

Also coming from the second half of the 17th century are the Hatton Garden Wall Hangings, six panels measuring about 4ft. by 9ft. They are embroidered with wool, in a fairly coarse stitch, in tent, brick, cross, croslet, and rococo, with a few French knots and some couched work.

Each panel has the same theme of flowers of huge size and fabulous ancestry clambering up carved stone pillars. These flowers are typical of 17th-century work—larger and more flamboyant than their predecessors, though the old favourites still appeared.

At the bases of the panels are miniature animals, weird in shape at times but always recognisable as elephant, lion, unicorn, leopard, dragon and a highly comic camel. A horse on one of the hangings is rather better proportioned than the other animals, presumably because the artist had more opportunity to observe horses. The upper reaches of the panels are embroidered prolifically with beautiful birds.

It would appear, however, that these charming hangings were not appreciated as they should have been. They were discovered languishing under several layers of wallpaper in a room in Hatton Garden (the street of jewellers) in London. Rescued and cleaned, they now decorate the walls of a typical room of the period in the Victoria and Albert Museum, London.

A very good example of the changing tastes is a long cushion cover of the early 17th century. Exotic flowers along with lions sporting rather ant-eater snouts surround the coat of arms of James I. The work is stiff and not as pleasing as the earlier embroideries, but the embroideress, Mary Hulton, was proud enough of it to sign the cushion cover in stitching more than an inch high. Mary Hulton was a prolific embroideress and several of her works are still intact. On the cushion cover she used silver-gilt, coloured wool and silk threads in long-armed cross, plaited and tent stitches.

Illustrating a different approach to the usual depiction of animals is a 17th-century Portuguese canvas embroidered carpet. In wool, using long-armed cross stitch throughout, it

A modern design, in which the background has been deliberately given more interest than the pine cone centre motif.

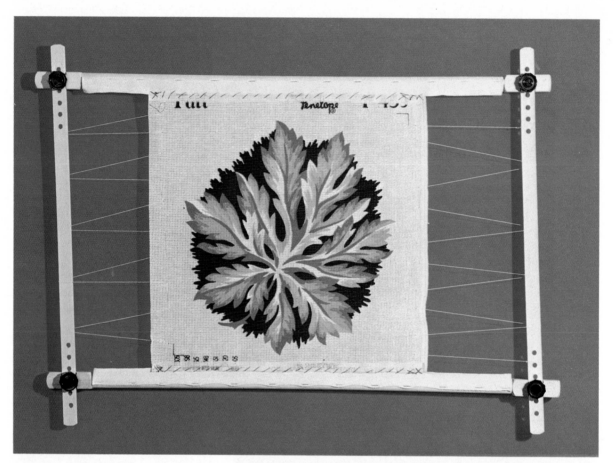

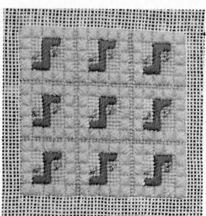

Top: work on a leader frame.
Above: example of a repeating motif (diaper pattern).
Right: a pattern in tent, cross, brick and star stitches suitable for a kneeler border (left) and examples of Florentine stitches, showing variations in stitch and threads. Plastic raffia has been used for bottom sample.

shows formalised birds and beasts, which are out of proportion to each other. Yet the rearing donkeys which fill corners are tremendously joyful and lovingly observed. This charming carpet is approximately 12ft. by 6ft. and is coloured bluey-green, beige, fawn, blue and deep blue—typical of Portuguese work of the period.

Books of this time were expensive and highly prized. They were treated with great respect and decorative bindings were embroidered for them. Often these bindings were of fragile materials, intricately decorated, and few of them have lasted. But canvas embroidered bindings were both handsome and long-wearing. One cover still in existence was made for a Geneva Bible published in 1610, inscribed: 'Elizabeth Illingworthe is the true owner of this Bible'. The actual embroidery is dated 1613. On one side it shows Jonah and the Whale—a rather bemused Jonah crawling on to a beach from the maw of a scaled and finned creature with the tail of a fish and the head and jaws of a crocodile. The reverse side shows the Sacrifice of Isaac. The embroidery is in tent stitch, using many-coloured silks.

An unusual portrait of Charles I as the central figure in the Judgement of Solomon was made in the mid-17th century. Tent is the main stitch, though many others are used, with silver and gold thread. This work represents the phase of Stuart embroidery which came before the exaggerated type of stump work which flourished from about 1650 to the 1680s.

In the 17th century pictorial embroidery, which earlier was put to practical purposes, now tended to be used more for pure decoration. Most pieces were framed and hung as pictures. Fine canvas embroidery was used for the earliest work, but later pictures were done in flat stitching and then in three-dimensional stump work using many materials and incorporating other objects.

Many more books of embroidery patterns were being published in the late 17th century, as is clear from so much repetition of closely similar designs on embroidered work of the period, especially on panels applied to small cabinets and trinket boxes. Messrs Peter Stent and John Overton published designs in the 1660s and 1670s. *The Needle's Excellency,*

Above and below: Spanish wall hangings, late 17th century. Canvas is embroidered with coloured silks in laid and couched work.

published by James Boler earlier in the century, was also much referred to for designs.

Two big new influences on embroidery at this time were Persian carpet patterns and the style of crewel work.

Geometric Persian patterns are reflected in 17th-century work throughout Europe. In Persia itself canvas embroidery work of the 16th to 18th centuries was almost entirely copied from carpet designs. The earliest surviving work is almost all divan covers or ceremonial cloths, sometimes in cross stitch, on loosely woven linen. In the 18th century the Persians made some very beautiful cushion covers, sometimes called Mongolian as well as Persian. As with the Elizabethans, cushions were not luxuries to them but essential home furnishings. Colour schemes were almost always predominantly black and yellow with some red, blue and green.

Crewel work—flat stitching in wool on twill-woven cotton and linen—became very popular towards the middle of the century. In fact crewel began to take over from canvas embroidery on such things as bed hangings. Some embroidery of this kind was done for the European market in India and China, and oriental touches began to creep into European design. An example of this is the Hatton Garden Hangings with their bold, exotic blooms, described above.

Early American work

Crewel wools were taken to America by the early settlers, along with embroidery techniques from many countries—all European methods were introduced but limited resources enforced adaptations. Long before the arrival of the settlers and explorers, the Indians in America had decorated skins—otter, beaver, sheep, doe, buck, elk and bison—with porcupine quills and beads. Shades of red, blue, green, purple, brown and white dye were obtained from native plants. The quills were couched with fine thread sir ew first in traditional geometric and stylised patterns, later in floral and other patterns.

Beads, made originally of crude minerals, seeds, horn, bone and shell were strung in short lengths and attached to skin or trade cloth by couching in solid areas of colour.

American crewel embroidery was far lighter than in England, and less influenced by Indian and Chinese fabrics. Floral designs were embroidered on clothes and on household articles.

Around this time fashions in furniture in all countries were also changing. Cushions on benches and window seats were superseded by individual straight-backed chairs. Seats and backs were upholstered in canvas embroidery. In the mid-century, design for this purpose tended to follow the style of Elizabethan cushion covers. But later examples show a rococo influence and flowers, though still very popular, were likely to be shown as an arrangement, complete with embroidered vase. A combination of wool and silk was popular, with Hungarian, tent, satin, split, long and short stitches being used on the same piece.

Return to practical embroidery

The first part of the 18th century was marked by a return to

MARY SMITH
HER WORK MADE
IN THE YEAR OF
OUR LORD

A sampler worked in cross and tent stitches in coloured silks on a woollen canvas; English, 18th century.

practical embroidery. There were fewer embroidered pictures, and less of the complicated samplers which young girls had been expected to work. However, one exception—probably by a child—is a charmingly unsophisticated picture of a fantastic house in an oak wood, made by a certain Elizabeth Haines in 1720. Tent, satin and encroaching satin stitches in silk were used on a woollen canvas.

Canvas work was particularly popular from the beginning of the century, and many lovely examples survive. Chairs were often upholstered with canvas embroidery. Wreaths of flowers

in a softer, more open style were in vogue as can be seen on a set of twenty chair covers of the early 18th century at the Victoria and Albert Museum, London. They were embroidered by Lady King, wife to Peter, First Baron King, Lord Chancellor. Wool and silk in tent stich were used.

In 1747 Prudence Nisbitt used tent and cross stitches in wool and silk for a charming chair seat. The simple design of flowers and leaves surrounding a shield (embroidered with her name) is strictly symmetrical.

Screens of every kind were popular and these were often decorated with canvas embroidered panels. The theatre, classics and country were all favourite themes for them. But whatever was depicted, bold flowers were almost invariably included.

Chinoiserie furniture, ornaments and decor were fashionable at the time, and a typical screen made in England about 1700 shows Chinese figures and landscape on a plain ground. Of the eleven people depicted on the canvas, only one has what could pass for a Chinese face. The others are a mixture of European and Indian, and one wide-eyed gentleman wears a typically Quaker hat! However it is an enchanting piece, worked in wool (mostly) and silk, with some details slightly padded.

A taste for Chinoiserie is reflected in canvas embroidered carpets of the century. Carpets of this kind came more into favour then and many beautiful examples still exist. The period of 1700–1750 produced the best needlework carpets ever made. Designs tended to be simpler and better integrated and the high quality of the work leads one to believe that much of it was done in commercial workshops.

The Hatfield House Carpet, property of the Marquess of Salisbury at Hatfield House, Hertfordshire, was made about 1740. Using fine wools and silks, it is entirely in tent stitch apart from some small detailing in French knots. Very fresh and colourful, it is packed with flowers and leaves on a dark ground, with a similarly patterned border on a red ground.

Examples of around 1765 usually show a rococo medallion as the centre piece.

Canvas work lost a good deal of popularity towards the end of the century. But other kinds of embroidery went out of favour too. Purely decorative pictures and portraits became the vogue. There was a tendency to make very careful, un-inspired copies of engravings, and needlework portraits were much admired.

Even the sampler became strictly stylised, and no longer the example of stitches and patterns that it once had been. Cross stitch verses were worked instead.

Berlin wool work

The most important needlework fashion in the 19th century was Berlin woolwork which swept through England and America and was tremendously popular for thirty years. Bright colours and sentimental subjects—pet dogs, pictures of royal pets, bouquets of roses, were the outstanding features.

Designs were copied from coloured patterns first published in Berlin about 1805, and imported in large quantities by a London shop in 1831. At first pictures were worked entirely

An example of 19th century Berlin work.

in cross and tent stitch with worsted wools, but soon details were added in clipped wool, cut-steel beads, jewels, pearls and sequins.

There was a great spate of books and periodicals on the subject and in her *Illuminated Book of Needlework* (published in 1847) Mrs Henry Owen starts off: 'Embroidery or as it is more often called Berlin woolwork . . . .

Eventually every conceivable small article, upholstery, rugs and carpets were all embroidered, until at last geometric patterns and softer colours began to appear again in the 1860s.

Forerunners of Berlin woolwork designs had appeared in Portugal at the end of the 18th century. One design showed a bouquet of flowers and a wreath; another a plate of food complete with knife and fork, glass and bottle of wine.

American women worked Berlin woolwork too, though they added coloured glass beads and finished with heavy silk cords, tassels, ribbons, bows and fringes. It was also worked on perforated cardboard for bookmarks, greeting cards and wall mottoes.

Other canvas embroidery of the period is a mixture of un-related styles and on the whole shows very little originality or understanding of design.

Much Berlin work was on household items such as carpets and chair covers. During the earlier part of the century—into the 1830s—design showed some restraint. Charming examples exist of a Queen Anne revival in canvas embroidered carpets.

But later carpets are rather less pleasing. In the Wilberforce House museum at Hull, England, is a stained glass window carpet. Cross stitch was used throughout in a pattern of

Gothic and rose windows filled with reds, greens, pinks, blues, ambers and purples.

Also at this time, huge floral carpets were made by groups of needlewomen in completely disparate squares and later stitched together. The Bishop Monk Victorian Carpet was presented in 1842 by the ladies of Gloucester to their bishop. Seventy-seven all-different panels were embroidered by seventy-seven ladies of varying taste and ability. The finished result is more curious than pleasing.

A somewhat similar piece made in 1845, known as a kettle-holder carpet, is made up of several small canvas squares in tent stitch. Here the motifs are even more different in style, yet somehow the work has an enchanting naivety.

Machinery was now in very strong competition with hands in the field of embroidery. Carpets, also machine-made, sounded the death knell for embroidered work. By 1900 white embroidery and embroidered dress materials were also mass-produced at low prices.

Reaction to both uninspired Victorian taste and impersonal machine work was led by architects and designers. William Morris designed many hangings and bed covers in bold flower and plant motifs, much of it based on 17th-century crewel work.

Art Needlework, inspired by William Morris's ideas, became very popular from 1870. Some canvas and crewel work of the period was also done by Art Needlework enthusiasts, both in contemporary and revised designs. Copies of 17th-century canvas embroideries were made with wools in faded colours to give them an aged appearance.

Art Nouveau needlework of all kinds was encouraged by the Glasgow School of Art towards the end of the century. Simple stitchery and disciplined style were the rule.

Canvas bag embroidered with wool;
mid 19th century.

This held good for the first twenty years of the 20th century, but then embroidery of all kinds went into another decline. Canvas embroidery, though still very popular, suffered from a lack of originality.

But fine canvas work has made a comeback in church furnishings, particularly in the production of kneelers.

Chelsea Old Church, London, was almost completely destroyed by a landmine during the 1939–1945 war. After its rebuilding, members of the congregation designed and embroidered about two hundred kneelers whose subjects were famous Chelsea residents of the past. Included is a set of over thirty embroideries telling the history of 16th-century Sir Thomas More and his family.

The Winchester Cathedral Broderers were formed in 1931 to furnish canvas embroideries for the choir. Five years' work resulted in a great series of cushions and kneelers which are an inspiration and model to cathedrals and churches in many countries.

Over two hundred embroideresses of varying ability worked on the Winchester Cathedral pieces, each being given work to suit her ability and experience. Today, despite hard wear, the work is still beautiful and well worth seeing.

Wells and Worcester Cathedrals and Southwell Minster all contain beautifully embroidered kneelers. At St David's Cathedral, Pembrokeshire, is a beautiful cushion made for the Queen's stall. It shows how rice stitch can be simply used to make an attractive background to a central design of a coat of arms.

STS Sir Winston Churchill, a modern tapestry embroidered picture, Penelope Design E/P457.

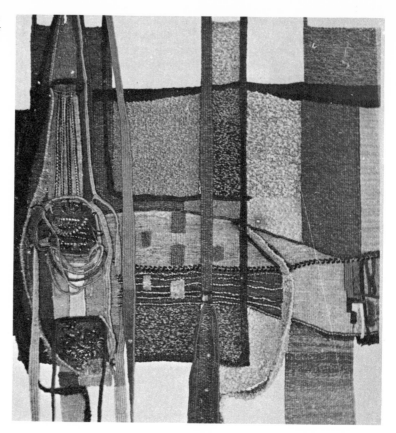

Rhythm of Blue Verticals, a modern woven wall hanging, with warp of cotton and weft of cotton, wool, horse-hair and metal industrial waste.

At Holyrood House, Edinburgh, is a canvas embroidered octagonal screen panel from the hand of the late Dowager Queen Mary. She was an enthusiastic embroideress and designed the panel herself. The pattern of flowers is early Victorian, whilst the octagonal frame round each bunch is more Edwardian. Known as the Holyrood Rose, it is a simple yet very attractive example of individual modern canvas embroidery.

The modern image

Today canvas embroidery has never presented so many different facets, so many possibilities to the needlewoman—and such a challenge. At one end of the scale there are now commercially produced needlework tapestry 'pictures', not dissimilar from the Victorian Berlin woolwork designs—these can provide a pleasant means of working with needle and thread. Alternatively, attractive wall hangings and pictures, fashion accessories, and traditional and elegant furnishings for the home, can all be successfully designed and made in canvas embroidery.

At the other end of the scale, exciting dramatic designs are being produced by students and artists in all parts of the world, but in America and Great Britain in particular: works using new techniques, new fibres and materials, and wonderful vivid ideas. No longer are discreet floral firescreens embroidered but vast abstract hangings which reflect today's trends, thoughts, and images. For canvas work can be as exciting, as varied, and as individual as any other art form.

tools and equipment

The basic requirements of canvas embroidery by way of tools, equipment and materials are, simply, yarn, canvas and needles. A frame is also useful although, depending on the type of work you do, not absolutely necessary. There are various other items which will help to make your work easier, and these are listed at the end of this chapter.

The choice of the three basic materials—yarn, canvas and needles—will depend naturally on the item you are making, and the purpose for which the finished design is intended. In the main however as tapestry work is used for items which have to withstand long and constant wear—e.g. chair seats, cushions, handbags, kneelers, and so forth—it is important that both yarn and canvas whether fine or coarse, are capable of surviving hard wear. The choice of stitches also is a contributory factor to the wearing qualities of a design: a stitch, for instance, which gives good solid coverage of canvas both on the back and front of the canvas will last a good deal longer than one where most of the thread is on the front of the canvas only.

Ideally, the fabric of the stitches should be thicker on the wrong side of the work to give a good thick padding for the

A selection of threads and materials suitable for canvas work.

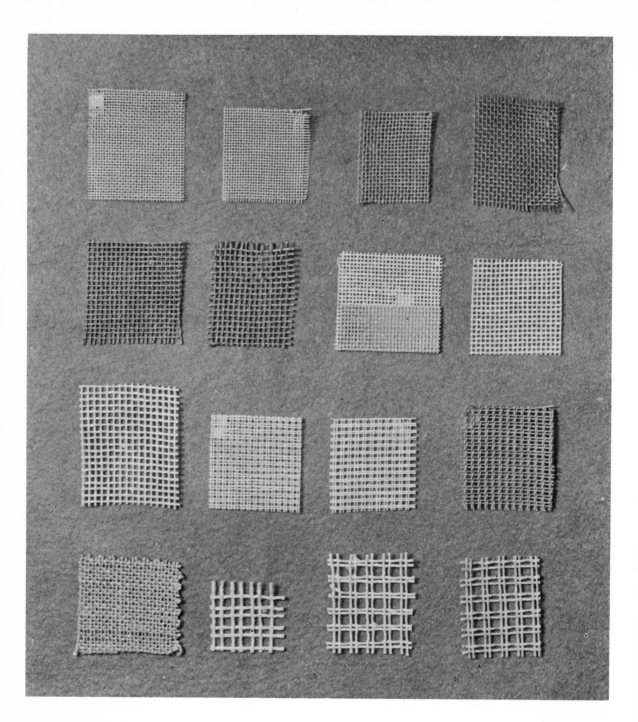

A selection of different canvases. Top row, left to right: single French canvases, 28, 24, 18 and 16 threads to the inch. 2nd row: French single, 14; French single, 12; English single, 18; English single, 12. 3rd row: raffia canvas, 10; Danish white, 12; English double (Penelope), 10; French double, 9. 4th row: flax canvas; rug canvas, 3; Smyrna canvas, 4; double canvas, 4.

canvas. Stitches which give this coverage to the canvas may use considerably more yarn than front-covering stitches, and be therefore more expensive to work initially, but in the long run in terms of durability this can be an economy.

YARNS TO CHOOSE

At one time it was customary to use silk, wool or linen threads for canvas work. Now however, thanks to the continued and ever-improving ranges of natural and synthetic threads, it is possible to use a very wide variety of threads indeed. So long as the yarn is a hardwearing one it is suitable for canvas work. This includes such diverse threads as raffia and sturdy rug wool, cotton and silk. Knitting wool is not particularly suitable as it will not survive constant wear and tear, but if it is used in conjunction with another yarn—such as a strong linen upholstery thread perhaps—then it can give satisfactory results. Most forms of weaving threads are suitable too.

It is worth experimenting with unusual and novelty yarns, and with different combinations of apparently dissimilar yarns. The traditional yarns however, and the ones with which it is best to begin are: tapestry (tapisserie) wool, crewel wool, and embroidery cottons. Tapestry wool and crewel wool are both made specially for canvas work, and are usually mothproof, with hardwearing qualities. Crewel wool can be used in single or multiple strands, using sufficient strands to cover canvas. The embroidery cottons—strand and pearl—can also be used in single or multiple strands. Tapestry wool however is always used only as a single thread.

All these yarns are available in a good range of colours, from the subtle tones of the conventional tapestry shades through to vivid colours suitable for modern embroidery.

Many novelty yarns—metal threads, threads with a special finish, even fine string—can all serve their purpose in a modern canvas embroidery.

Whichever thread you choose to work with, it is essential that you buy sufficient at a time to see you through a complete design. Dye lots of yarns do vary—the difference may be barely discernible when you buy the yarn but when made up can result in an unattractive patchiness. If you are working on a design you yourself have created (rather than from a published pattern where quantities of thread required will be quoted), then work a small section of the proposed design first. If the pattern is to include repeats of a motif, then work one motif so you can estimate with reasonable accuracy how much yarn you will require.

Whichever yarn you choose for basic stitches it should never be finer than the threads of the canvas or the background of the canvas will show through the stitches in your design.

The Three Kings, a modern canvas work picture using a variety of stitches and threads, including metal and gold thread.

CANVAS

Although in your finished work the canvas will—or should be—completely covered by thread, it is as important to choose a good quality canvas as it is a good thread, for this is what gives substance and longwearing qualities to your finished work. Again, it is a false economy to buy cheap canvas—except perhaps for your first practise samplers, unless of course you intend to frame them and keep them for posterity!

As a rule the cheaper canvases are made from cotton; the better quality ones from polished linen threads which are smooth and nicely rounded. Canvas made from this type of thread is firm and does not readily twist out of shape.

Canvas is a woven fabric consisting of a number of vertical threads (the warp threads) criss-crossed with a number of horizontal threads (the weft threads). There are basically two kinds of canvas: single-thread canvases known as plain or congress, and double-thread canvases, sometimes known as Penelope canvas. In the double-thread canvases, warp and weft threads are arranged in pairs.

For practise purposes, the single-thread canvases are easier to work with. The double-thread canvases are useful for more intricate work where tent stitch and trammed tent stitch, for instance, are to be combined on the one piece—the trammed tent stitches are worked over the double threads of the canvas; for the tent stitches (the fine stitches) the double threads are opened up and stitches worked over single threads.

Both single and double canvases are available in a wide range of mesh sizes—that is, the degree by which the woven threads are spaced out. A wide mesh will give fewer warp and weft threads to the inch; a fine mesh will give considerably more.

In single canvas the mesh is determined by the number of threads to the inch; in double canvas it is specified by the number of holes to the inch. In single canvas, mesh sizes range from 10 to about 32 threads to the inch: 10 threads to the inch is a good coarse mesh to work practise samplers on as stitches are easy to see and to control.

A mesh of about 14 to 16 threads to the inch is a good everyday weight for most purposes—for making kneelers, cushions, wall panels, handbags. For more intricate work, such as an evening bag or a belt, a finer mesh should be used.

Rug canvas is also available which has only 3, 4 or 5 holes to the inch—this is splendid for making big-scale hangings and other bold designs. Of course a suitable thick yarn—such as rug wool—has to be used. In all cases yarn and canvas must complement each other, and at no time should the threads of the canvas ever be thicker than the yarn used, otherwise you will not get good coverage. If you wish to use a fine wool on a coarse mesh, then several strands together will have to be used. Knotted work—rugs, for instance—should be worked on a soft linen base, rather than the rigid canvas.

All grades and mesh sizes of canvas are available in a choice of widths to suit different purposes, from 18in. to 36in. English canvas is usually white; French canvas is a pleasant browny beige colour; raffia canvas is the cheapest and ideal for practising stitches on. Winchester canvas—now more usually called flax canvas—is the traditional canvas on which to work kneelers and hassocks. Canvas with 4 holes to the inch is sometimes known as Smyrna canvas.

NEEDLES

A true tapestry needle has a rounded blunt point which passes through the holes of the canvas easily without forcing the threads apart, and without splitting the threads. It also has a large oval eye which can be easily threaded with fairly thick wool—ideally, the needle should be large enough to take the thread you are using comfortably, but not so large that it opens up the squares of the canvas.

As with ordinary sewing needles, tapestry needles are available in a range of sizes to suit different types of work.

The sizes most popular for medium-weight designs are Nos. 18 and 19. For fine work, choose a No. 24. For coarse work, chose a No. 13.

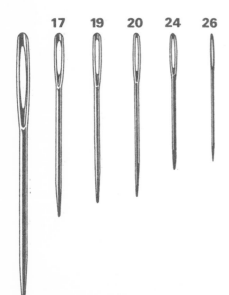

17   19   20   24   26

FRAMES

If you intend to work only in straight stitches, following the warp and weft of the canvas, then a frame is not necessary. It is enough to roll and weight the canvas as you work (see working methods, page 33). However by not using any of the vast number of diagonal and cross stitches, you will limit the scope of your work, so a good frame is a worthwhile investment. Round embroidery frames are not suitable for canvas work as they pull the canvas out of shape. A square or rectangular frame should always be used. This is a relatively simple piece of equipment which can if you wish be made at home.

Leader frame.

There are various sizes and types of commercially made frames available, but the principle of each is the same: two horizontal rollers are each covered with webbing or tape to which the top and bottom of your canvas is attached. These rollers slot or screw into wooden side laths.

The object of the frame is to keep your work stretched tautly at all times and in all directions to prevent the canvas being pulled out of shape by the continued use of stitches in one direction. The top and bottom of canvas is attached to the webbing, and the sides are laced to the side laths of the frame, then the canvas is stretched to the necessary degree of tautness.

The width of your work should never exceed the measurement of the webbing or tape on the horizontal rollers. The length is adaptable as the canvas can be rolled and adjusted depending on the flexibility of the frame. Frames with screw-fitting side laths give greater flexibility than those with peg fittings.

Travel frame.

The governing feature of the frame therefore is the actual length of webbing fitted to it, and it is by this measurement that frames are usually sold. Various sizes are available from 18in. to 36in. A 26 or 27in. size is a good useful general purpose size to choose. It is always possible to adapt a large size frame for a smaller size canvas, but not possible to adapt a small frame to take a larger canvas.

There are four principal types of frame available.

Leader frame

This is a simple rectangular frame which needs to be supported at a comfortable working height in order to leave your hands free to stitch. This can be done by resting the frame against the edge of a table—if the bottom of the frame can be wedged on the arms of the chair you are sitting in, this gives an ideal working position. This type of frame is usually available with 18, 24 or 27in. webbing.

Travel frame

This is useful as an auxiliary frame if you want to carry your work around with you to do on a train, in the garden or on the beach. But a travel frame is not to be recommended for constant home use. It is a neat, rectangular frame which offers a choice of 12, 24 or 27in. webbing, but the total depth is only 12in. Therefore if your work is to be longer than 12in., each time the canvas is re-rolled into position the lacing at the sides will have to be redone. The frame is useful for small pieces of work.

Table frame.

Floor frame.

Table frame
This is a self-supported frame which can be stood on a table top or working surface. Screw fittings adjust the frame to give the precise slant you prefer. Available in a good range of sizes.

Tapestry floor frame
This is by far the most convenient of all types of frame—it is a free-standing and fully adjustable frame, similar in principle to the artist's easel. It can be placed anywhere you wish to work, with canvas permanently in position ready for you to continue stitching when you have the opportunity. Available in a range of sizes, up to 36in.

There are also frames available which are specially designed for invalids and disabled people. The frames can be comfortably used in an armchair or even in bed. The action of this type of frame differs from the normal tapestry frame in that you can see the next stitch hole on the back of the canvas instead of having to feel for it.

A simple home-made frame can be constructed from four suitable lengths of wood nailed together to form a picture frame shape. Your work is then tacked with drawing pins to this base. The frame should be slightly bigger than your canvas so the canvas has to be stretched to fit.

OTHER USEFUL TOOLS AND EQUIPMENT
Scissors. A good strong, well-sharpened pair suitable for cutting canvas, plus a small pair of embroidery scissors for cutting threads.
Drawing pins. For tacking work to a home-made frame, and for pinning out canvas to stretch it.
Pins. Good-quality steel ones.
Waterproof Indian ink. For painting on designs to your canvas.
Tracing paper. For planning and transferring designs.
Tape measure. Preferably a steel measure with inches and centimetre markings.
Blotting paper. For stretching canvas after design is worked.
A piece of clean wood. To be used for stretching canvas. The wood should be sufficiently soft to take pins easily—fibreboard or a piece of cork is ideal. The size of the surface will depend on the size of items you are likely to want to make.
Tweezers. Useful for unpicking work.
Graph paper and sharp pencils. For plotting your own designs.
Fine string or button thread. For lacing canvas to the frame.
Tape—in $\frac{1}{2}$in. and 1in. widths. For framing-up canvas and binding edges where necessary.

working methods

There are a number of preliminary preparations to be dealt with before you can reach the exciting stage of actually working the stitches in your canvas work design.

The most important of these is the preparation of the canvas, and—if you are using a frame—mounting it on to your frame, a process known as 'framing-up'.

PREPARING THE CANVAS

Cut canvas to about 3in. larger all round than the finished size of the design you intend to work.

It is important that the canvas is always used the right way up—i.e. with the selvedges running vertically. There are however occasions such as with a very wide design, perhaps for a stool top, when it may be necessary to mount the canvas with selvedges at the top and bottom. But this is the exception to the general rule.

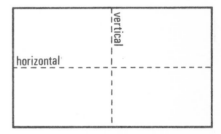

Measure out the centre of the canvas both horizontally and vertically, and mark these centre lines with a row of basting stitches. Use ordinary sewing cotton to work basting, choosing two different contrasting colours—one for the horizontal basting, one for the vertical. This will also help to identify which way up the canvas goes. You can, for instance, always use a red cotton to mark the horizontal centre line, and a blue cotton to mark the vertical centre line. Choose colours which show up clearly against the canvas.

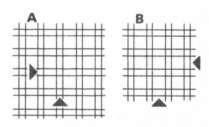

If you are using a double thread canvas sometimes your centre lines may occur between a pair of threads, in which case work your basting exactly between the threads (see diagram A). If the centre however occurs on a line of holes then work your basting stitches along this line (see diagram B). It is important to mark the centre lines as accurately as possible.

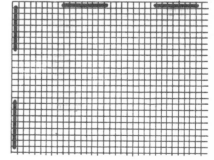

If you are working from a chart it may be helpful to mark out your threads (or holes) in groups of eight or ten (according to the graph you are following). Use a third colour of cotton (i.e. different from horizontal and vertical basting stitches already worked), work a line of stitches along the top edge of your canvas, taking the stitches alternately over and under ten (or eight) threads. Work a similar line of stitches down the left-hand side edge of canvas.

Now fold back $\frac{1}{2}$in. turnings at top and bottom edges of canvas, and tack these to keep them in place. Similarly make $\frac{1}{2}$in. turnings on side edges of canvas. Bind these with a length of tape, 1in. wide. Either machine stitch the tape to the canvas, or sew it in place by hand with a strong cotton. Your canvas is now ready for framing-up, if you are using a frame, or for beginning work, if you are not using a frame.

IF YOU DO NOT USE A FRAME . . .

Only designs worked entirely in straight stitches (following the warp and weft of the canvas) can satisfactorily be worked without a frame. Any form of diagonal stitches pulls the canvas out of shape, unless securely mounted on a frame to compensate for the distortion.

If you are not using a frame, the end of your canvas should be weighted with dressmakers' weights, and each time you stop work the canvas should be carefully rolled—never folded. While you work roll the top part of the canvas down to the section being held for stitching.

As you roll up a worked section of canvas, it is a good idea to slip in a sheet of tissue paper to protect your work.

FRAMING-UP PREPARED CANVAS

The instructions for framing-up apply to all types of frame. The centre point of the binding on the frame should be marked. This can be marked permanently with an indelible marking ink or a waterproof Indian ink, as it will always be necessary to know the midway point on the rollers.

Sew top of prepared canvas with overcasting stitches securely to top roller; bottom edge of prepared canvas to bottom roller. Match the centre point of rollers to the centre basting stitches on the canvas. Use a strong cotton thread to stitch, working from centre point outwards on each side. If you try to work the seam all at once from one side to the other, you may well find at the end that the centre points are out of alignment.

Wind surplus canvas—if any—round the rollers, then assemble the rollers in frame, adjusting screws or pegs so that the canvas is stretched tautly from top to bottom.

Now the sides of the canvas are laced to either side of the frame. Use thin string or four strands of button thread for the lacing. Take the lacing through the taped side edge of canvas and round side strut of frame at about 1 in. intervals. When canvas is tightly laced in position tie each end of lacing thread securely to the frame to keep it in place. As your work proceeds, if you have to roll and unroll new sections of canvas it will of course be necessary to re-lace each new section in a similar way to the frame. Sometimes lacing will become slack as you work, and will have to be re-tightened from time to time to maintain a constant tension.

BEGINNING WORK

It is important, as with any other form of handicraft or needlework, that you work in a comfortable position, and in a good light.

If you are using a floor frame, then adjust the height of the frame to suit your chair height. Never make do either with poor working conditions or inadequate light: the result can only be inferior work, and wasted time and effort. Canvas embroidery, above all, should never be rushed: it is a leisurely, relaxed pastime, a legacy from days when needlework was a gentle and pleasurable means of whiling away uncrowded hours. The activity was paramount; the end-product incidental.

The basic method of working applies to every variety of stitch, whether worked over a single thread of the canvas, or over

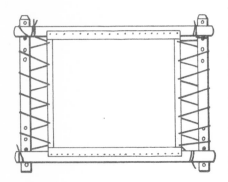

Canvas correctly framed-up, and embroidery under way.

Above: footstool with a traditional floral design.
Left: a modern picture, using a great variety of stitches.

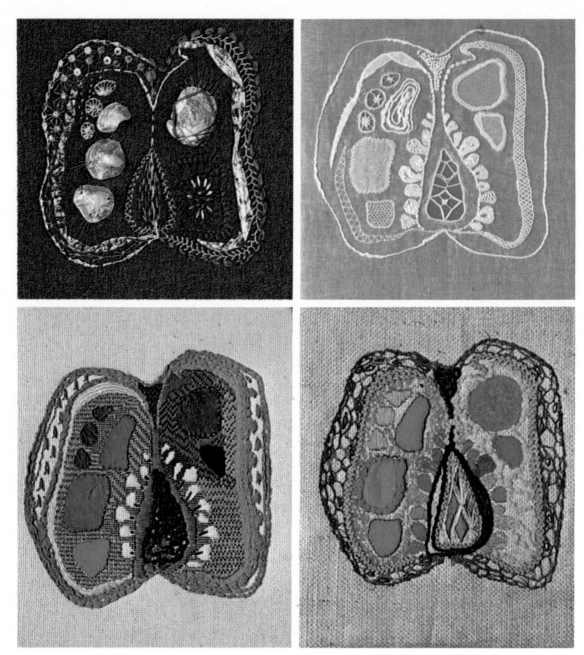

One motif—four different embroidery
techniques.

several together. The method is this: with one hand on top of the canvas, insert the needle downwards into the canvas, and pull it through with the other hand. With the same hand, insert the needle upwards into the canvas, and pull it through with the hand still on top (which hand is used for which process is a matter of personal preference). Never pull stitches too tightly. With practice, speed and regularity of stitch will soon be achieved. Wherever possible, always take the thread up through an empty hole and down through a hole which already has a thread in it.

There are two basic methods of starting a new thread (either at the beginning of your work, or when joining in a new thread).

Method 1. Make a knot at the end of your thread, then take it through canvas from the right to the wrong side, an inch or two away from the point where you wish stitching to begin. Bring needle back through to the right side at the point of stitching. Continue with design. The thread will be securely held in place as stitches are worked so that eventually the knot may be cut off, the loose end of thread pulled gently to the back of the canvas, and darned into the wrong side of stitching.

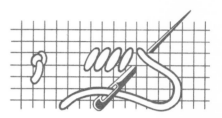

Method 2. Begin work at point of stitching, bringing needle through from the wrong to the right side of work. Leave about 1 in. of thread at the back, and carefully hold this end against the back of the canvas. Work over it with the first few stitches. Once it is secure you may stop holding it.

With either method, it is important to avoid making too many joins near the same point in the design, as this would make the work unattractively ridged and uneven.

At the end of a length of yarn, or end of a design, leave a few inches of yarn and carefully darn in about 1 in to the back of stitching, trimming away the remainder.

If you are working on a design which uses a number of different colours rather than having constantly to finish off threads and start again, when you have worked a few stitches in

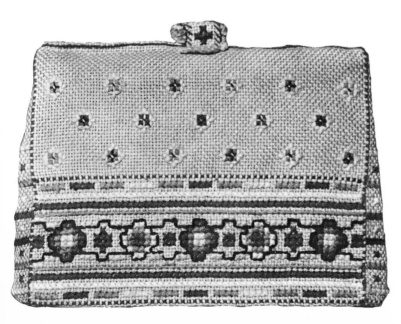

Tea cosy worked in canvas stitches on a coarse fabric ground.

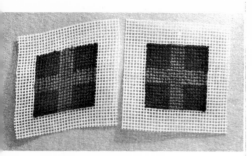

Above: tent stitch worked correctly in diagonal rows (right), worked incorrectly in rows and hence pulled badly out of shape (left). Below are the reverse sides of the same samples.

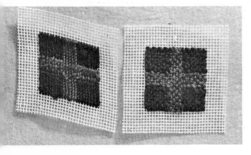

Above: untrammed tent stitch, with canvas ground showing through. Below: trammed tent stitch, with canvas closely covered.

one colour bring the needle through to the front of work an inch or two away from where you are working and leave it there ready to be picked up when that colour is next required.

Never work with a thread longer than about 16in. The constant friction of thread against canvas soon wears thin patches in a too-long thread which would result in patchy finished work. Change the position of the yarn in the needle occasionally to avoid the friction of the needle eye.

If the thread becomes twisted while you are working, allow the needle to hang down and the thread will untwist itself, or take the needle back down the thread to the surface of the work and bring it back.

IMPORTANCE OF TENSION

As with knitting or crochet, or any other form of needlework where an allover fabric is created, it is essential that you maintain an even tension to your stitching. This is why before you embark on a finished design, you should practise the stitches you will use in the design until you are sufficiently familiar with them to work to a regular rhythm.

Work stitches neither too loose nor too tight. They must cover the canvas completely and bed evenly together to form a smooth texture.

Where a stitch is made up of a series of individual stitches, it is best always to work these individual stitches in the same order. Make sure background stitches are worked in the same direction as those worked for the design section. Never work in even blocks of stitching.

If you are working a large area in tent stitch, you will get a much more even texture and a more hardwearing fabric if you work in diagonal rows rather than horizontal ones (see page 62 for more detailed instructions).

TRAMMED STITCHES

For most forms of upholstery and any work where hardwearing qualities are particularly important, you will get a rich appearance to your work plus an extremely hardwearing sturdy fabric if you first 'tram' the canvas: this tramming is an important canvas work technique which consists of laying down long horizontal stitches across the areas of the canvas. The canvas stitches are then worked over the trammed stitches, thus giving a double layer of thread, ensuring complete coverage of the canvas ground, and giving an attractive almost 'padded' appearance to the finished work.

The trammed stitches, which are really similar to basting stitches, are worked to match the colour of the finished design and in a similar thread. Almost any canvas work stitch will benefit from being worked over a trammed surface, but the technique is particularly suitable for tent stitch backgrounds on double thread canvas.

There are several methods of working trammed stitches. The following give three possible methods:

Method 1. Single stitch tramming. Where the area to be trammed is not wider than 5in., it is sufficient to take separate single stitches from the left-hand side of the area across to the right-hand side. Bring the needle through from back to front of

Cross stitch sampler, late 19th century.

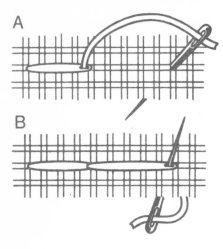

work between a pair of horizontal threads, then take the thread horizontally from left to right across area and through from front to back of work.

Method 2. Split trammed stitch. This is suitable for large areas where tramming is required—for instance, for backgrounds. Begin as for single stitch tramming, bringing thread from the back to the front of work at a point where a pair of vertical threads cross a pair of horizontal threads. Carry thread horizontally across work for a distance not exceeding 5in., and then take thread through to the back of work at a similar crossing of canvas threads (A). Now bring the thread back to front of work one vertical thread to the left on the same line, through stitch just made, thus forming a split stitch (B). Continue in this way across the area requiring tramming. When working several rows of tramming, stitches should be worked in such a way that they do not start or finish at the same pair of vertical threads. You will need to stagger the stitches in order to avoid this.

Vary lengths of stitching from 3 to 5in. Tramming must always cross the centre of canvas—never start or finish at this point.

Method 3. Vertical tramming. When working vertically—for instance, for outlines of areas—and tramming is required, take a short trammed stitch across an intersection of the canvas threads, then work required canvas stitch. When stitch is complete bring thread down between next pair of horizontal threads and immediately to the left of the vertical threads, take another tramming stitch across the vertical threads, and then work canvas stitch. Continue in this way.

Working tramming and half cross stitch concurrently

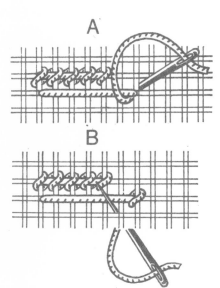

For blocks of half cross stitches where tramming is required, begin by bringing thread through from the wrong to the right side of work, at the right-hand side of area to be worked, and through a pair of horizontal threads. Take a straight tramming stitch horizontally across area from right to left, and take thread to the back of work immediately to the left of an intersection of the horizontal and vertical threads of the canvas, and through the horizontal threads as before. Bring thread back to the right side of work immediately below this point. Now work half cross stitch from left to right over the trammed stitch just worked. When the end of the stitch is reached, bring thread back through to the front of work between the horizontal threads immediately below the row just completed. In a similar way, take another tramming stitch across work from right to left, then work half cross stitches from left to right over this stitch. Trammed tent stitch may be worked in a similar way (see diagram A and B, left) but in this case work tramming stitches from left to right, tent stitch from right to left.

ORDER OF WORK

As a general rule, if a design consists of a background area and a centre design section, tramming if required will be worked first of all, then the centre design section will be worked, and finally the background is completed. For an allover design, it is usual to work from the centre outwards. Any areas still not covered when the design is complete can be filled in with small stitches.

However to make work less tedious, it can be an advantage

occasionally to break the rules! Instead of leaving all the background until the end, fill in small sections as you go along—in fact if the background is started, and left with needle and thread in position, you can do a few stitches of this almost mechanical part of the design whenever you have an odd moment to spare.

IF THINGS GO WRONG...

Even the most experienced needlewoman makes mistakes, or miscalculates or has the occasional disaster. If you really have got into a complete muddle, either by miscounting the threads of the canvas, or by using the wrong stitching or colours, the only answer—however disheartening it might be—is to unpick your work and do that section again. Use small embroidery scissors for clipping the threads you want to remove, taking great care not to clip through the canvas itself, then use tweezers to remove the cut threads one by one.

If despite careful framing-up or weighting, your canvas does become puckered as work proceeds, try dampening the wrong side of the canvas sparingly, cover with a dry pressing cloth, and quickly and lightly pass a hot iron over the puckered area. If a first application is not sufficient, repeat the process.

More serious puckering may be corrected when you stretch the canvas prior to making-up into finished item (see page 63). If on completion of a design, you find there are tiny areas of the canvas ground showing through you can remedy this by going over the stitches again with the same thread, and so giving the canvas double coverage.

the stitches you will use

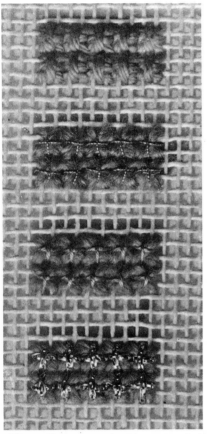

Above: Smyrna or double cross stitch worked with a variety of different threads.
Below: rice stitch samples worked with different threads and different canvases.

To many people, tapestry needlework means cross stitch and tent stitch—and little else. It might therefore come as some surprise to the novice canvas embroideress to learn of the almost limitless number of stitches which are available to her. Many of these are traditional stitches, used to work particular patterns and styles of canvas work; others have been 'devised' by needlewomen since the art of canvas embroidery was first discovered. There is virtually no limitation to the stitches you can use: the only limitation is in fact your own prowess—and imagination!

Although you will probably work your first samplers and experimental designs in the basic stitches—perhaps cross stitch in one of its many variations, and some of the simple straight stitches such as Hungarian or Parisian, do not neglect the other 'fancier' stitches. In fact the quicker you can become familiar with the different stitching techniques, and understand the characteristics of each, and the particular effects which can be achieved, the quicker will you become an accomplished canvas embroideress and go on to create exciting designs for yourself. Learn to know and understand as many stitches as possible and you will be able to 'paint' with them and create different textures just as an artist paints with oils or water colours.

Try out each one of the following stitches. Some you may find do not appeal so much as others, so you will no doubt eliminate them from your stitch vocabulary—canvas embroidery, after all, is a personal art—there is no need to use a particular stitch if you do not care for it just because it happens to be a traditional one.

A knowledge of stitches, techniques and the canvas itself can also be quickly acquired by trying each stitch in different yarns, and on different canvas types—it is surprising how the same stitch can take on a totally different appearance worked in a variety of threads—see illustrations left and below. Experiment with different yarn colours, even within the same stitch—for instance, by working alternate rows of different colours, or if a stitch consists of a number of individual stitches work some of these in a contrast colour (e.g. rice stitch lends itself well to experimenting with contrast threads and colours). It is also interesting to combine different thread types together using double or even triple thicknesses, provided of course the mesh

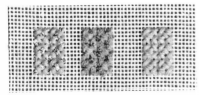

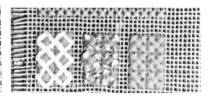

*Sampler in which a great variety of
stitches give textural interest.*

of the canvas is a suitable size. This all helps to give a new dimension to a particular stitch.

Once you have a fair understanding of a number of stitches, try combining several together on the same canvas—outline your design on paper first, if you wish, or 'draw' directly on your canvas with your stitches. A shape can be roughly outlined on the canvas with basting stitches to serve as a guide.

Do not be afraid to experiment or be worried in case your design is not good. The only way you can learn is by trial and error. There is one important rule to bear in mind all the time you are working, and this applies as much to experimental work as it does to ambitious finished designs: every part of the canvas background must be completely covered by thread. Upright stitches normally need thicker thread than diagonal stitches if the canvas is not to show through between stitches. Sometimes if the canvas does show through between rows of stitches, this can be remedied by working a line of back stitches.

A single thread canvas is the best to practise on (unless you want to combine tent stitch and trammed tent stitch in the same design—see page 62). For first samplers and stitch experimenting, a coarse canvas such as raffia canvas with ten threads to the inch will make your stitches easy to work and to see. Progress from this to a single thread canvas with 14 or 16 threads to the inch.

Do not work on too big a piece of canvas at the same time—better to have a number of small sample pieces than one over-large piece. An oblong of canvas measuring about 12in. by 9in. is a good practise size.

If you are not working on a frame then all the stitches you use will have to be the straight ones—the stitches which follow the direction of warp and weft canvas threads. There is a good variety of straight stitches to choose from: brick, straight gobelin, Parisian, satin, Hungarian and Florentine. Eye and star stitches also keep their shape well without a frame.

Of course if you do use a frame, then the whole range of stitches is then available to you. A very important point to

Above and right: experiments in stitching and design effects. A piece of canvas can be treated like a design notebook. Always have needle and thread ready to 'note' down new ideas.

remember, and one which may entail some careful preliminary counting, is that all stitches do not cover the same unit of canvas threads. Shapes should dovetail together inconspicuously at the edges. One or two tent or gobelin stitches often help to fill in tiny gaps when necessary.

The stitch dictionary which follows is presented alphabetically. For practise purposes however, it is best to start with the range of cross stitches and variations, and gobelin stitch and its variations, and then go on to the other stitches in any order you wish. In no time at all you will be inventing your own stitches.

Note. In most of the photographs which illustrate the stitches in this section, a thinner yarn has been used than would normally be chosen for the canvas mesh, in order that the construction of the stitches can be clearly seen. Similarly, in some cases the stitches and canvas threads as shown in the diagrams have been opened up for the sake of clarity where normally there would be dense coverage of the canvas by the stitches.

ALGERIAN EYE

This is a small close stitch which can quickly become bulky if too thick a thread is used. It is worked diagonally therefore any colour change will be in diagonal rows. The complete stitch covers a square of 4 horizontal and 4 vertical threads of the canvas, although each individual stitch is worked over only 2 threads. Begin by bringing needle through from back to front of canvas in centre of square. Work 8 double stitches to form a star shape. Begin with the top upright stitch, working the stitch twice before moving to the left and working top left diagonal stitch. Continue in this way, moving to the left for each stitch, working twice into each hole and pulling stitches tightly to emphasise the centre hole. The last stitch in the first eye will therefore come from the centre to top right-hand corner. When this double stitch is complete, bring needle through centre of next square of canvas where the stitch is to be worked. Continue in this way.

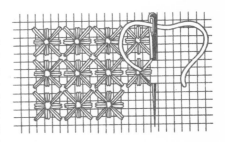

ALGERIAN PLAITED

This is similar to closed herringbone stitch on fabric. In its finished appearance it is also like plait stitch (see page 58) but is worked in a different way. Begin at top left-hand corner of area where stitching is to appear, and bring needle through at this point. Take a diagonal stitch down across 6 horizontal threads and 4 vertical threads to the right. Bring needle back through 3 vertical threads to the left, then take an upward diagonal stitch over 6 horizontal threads and 5 vertical threads to the right. Bring needle back through 3 vertical threads to the left. Continue in this way.

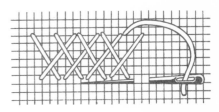

BRICKING OR BRICK

Also sometimes called Alternating Stitch.

Stitches are upright so will not pull canvas out of shape, and they can be worked over 3 or 4 threads, depending on depth required. Work first row from left to right, taking straight vertical stitches over 4 horizontal threads of the canvas. Bring needle through to right side of canvas at lower point of each

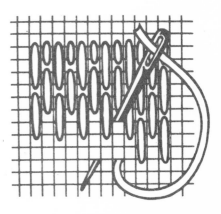

stitch, and work stitch upwards. Work stitches between alternate pairs of vertical threads. When the row is complete, work 2nd row from right to left, working stitches in the spaces between stitches of previous row to give an interlocked appearance. If stitches are being worked over 4 threads, then drop down 2 threads from previous row, and work stitches from bottom to top over 4 threads as before. If stitches are being worked over 3 threads, then only drop down one thread for 2nd row and work stitches over 3 threads as before. Continue in this way to form a solid interlocked area of stitching. This is a good stitch to use for shading, as colours can be changed in each row, to give an attractive merging of shades. If you wish to use the stitch for a background, and need coverage to the edge of the canvas, the first row should be worked with stitches alternately taken over 4 threads, then 2, working across all threads in the row. Thereafter continue in alternate sequence. The last row of the work will similarly require stitches all the way across, worked alternately long and short to fill in the area.

BYZANTINE

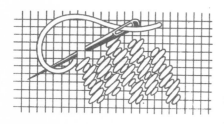

A useful diagonal stitch for covering an area of canvas quickly and effectively. It is worked over 4 horizontal and 4 vertical threads. Bring needle through at lower left-hand point where stitch is to occur then take needle 4 horizontal threads up and 4 vertical threads to the right. It is usual to arrange Byzantine stitches in 'steps' as shown in the diagram, with 6 stitches to each step. Colours may be changed with each row, if wished, or all rows worked in the same colour, and a contrast colour introduced with a line of back stitches between rows of Byzantine stitches (this also helps to hide the canvas between rows, if coverage is not good).

CASHMERE

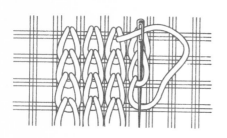

Each unit in this stitch consists of 3 individual stitches—one stitch worked over one intersection of the canvas threads, and 2 stitches each worked over 2 intersections of the canvas threads. Work from left to right in diagonal rows, moving one thread to the right for each new block of stitches. In each block, the lower tip of each individual stitch should fall one below the other—see diagram.

CHAIN

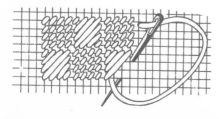

Bring needle out at top of area where chain is to appear. Hold down the thread with left thumb and insert needle into the mesh where the needle was first brought through and make a straight downward stitch behind one horizontal thread of the canvas. Bring needle through, keeping working thread under the needle point. Continue in this way, always inserting needle into the same mesh of the canvas as where it last emerged. Work in vertical rows from top to bottom.

CHEQUER

This is composed of 6 tent stitches (see page 61) and 7 diagonal stitches (see page 50) worked in alternate blocks. Each individual block of stitches covers 4 horizontal and 4 vertical threads of the canvas. Sixteen tent stitches are therefore contained in each tent stitch block; diagonal stitches are worked in graduated lengths to fill area, each stitch in turn covering 1, 2, 3, 4, 3, 2 and 1 intersections of the canvas threads. It is best to work rows diagonally, working all the tent stitch blocks first, then returning to the beginning and filling in remaining areas with diagonal stitch blocks. One colour may be used throughout, or 2 toning or contrasting shades used.

CROSS STITCH
An important group of stitches.

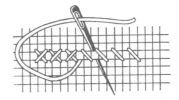

The **basic cross stitch** can be worked over one intersection of the canvas threads, or over 2, 3 or more vertical and horizontal threads. The first 'arm' of each cross should be worked from lower right-hand corner up to top left-hand corner. To complete the stitch, bring thread out at bottom left-hand corner and take stitch over the stitch already worked to top right-hand corner. Although horizontal rows of stitches can be worked by making only the first arm of the each cross in the first row, then working the 2nd arm on the return journey, in order to prevent distortion of the canvas and to maintain an even tension, it is better to complete each stitch before moving to the next. Stitches may be worked in horizontal rows (from left to right, or right to left), or as a further safeguard against distortion of the canvas, they can be worked in diagonal rows.

Alternating cross
Oblong cross stitches worked over 3 horizontal and 1 vertical threads of the canvas are worked first, leaving one vertical thread between each, then small basic cross stitches are worked between each oblong stitch, over the centre intersection. In the 2nd row, the oblong cross stitches are worked to fit between oblong stitches of previous row, then small basic crosses are worked between these oblong cross stitches. Continue in this way.

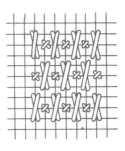

Diagonal cross
This stitch is composed of 3 small stitches (instead of 2 as most of the other cross stitches', and is worked in diagonal rows from bottom right up to top left of area to be covered. Each complete stitch covers 4 horizontal threads and 4 vertical threads of the canvas. Bring needle out between centre 2 vertical threads and immediately below bottom horizontal thread of the area where stitch is to appear. Take a straight upward stitch across 4 horizontal threads and bring needle back through at starting point. Now take a diagonal upward stitch to the right of 2 intersections of the canvas threads, and bring needle back through 4 vertical threads to the left. Complete the stitch by taking a straight horizontal stitch from left to right across the vertical stitch already worked and over 4 vertical threads. Continue in this way.

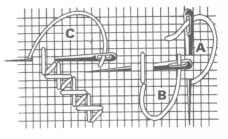

Double straight cross
This consists of a straight cross stitch worked over 4 threads held down in the centre by a basic cross over 2 threads. Work rows so stitches of one row fit between stitches of previous row.

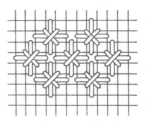

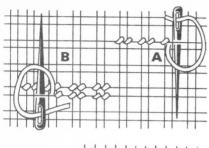

Half cross

This is simply the first half of the complete cross stitch and is useful for working when the thread is too thick for a complete cross stitch. It may be worked either trammed or untrammed (see page 38), and from right to left, or left to right. To work trammed half cross stitch, you must use double thread canvas. See page 40 for detailed working instructions.

Large and straight cross

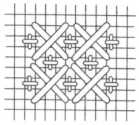

Work basic cross stitches over 4 by 4 threads, and fit straight cross stitches over 2 by 2 threads in between each pair of basic crosses.

Double back cross or basket

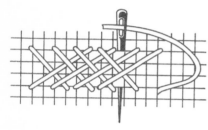

This closely interwoven stitch is worked to a depth of 4 horizontal threads. Working from left to right, bring needle out on lower line 4 threads to the right of point where row of stitches is to begin. Take an upward diagonal stitch over 4 horizontal threads of the canvas, and 4 vertical threads to the left. Bring needle out 4 horizontal threads immediately below. Now take a diagonal stitch 4 threads up and 6 vertical threads to the right, and bring needle out 4 threads immediately below. Continue in this way.

Long-armed cross

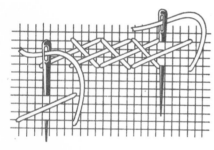

Sometimes called plaited Slav or long-legged cross.

Work from left to right. First diagonal stitch is taken from bottom left-hand corner up 4 horizontal threads, and across 8 vertical threads to the right. Bring needle out 4 horizontal threads immediately below. Then make 2nd arm of cross 4 threads up and 4 vertical threads to the left. Bring needle back 4 threads immediately below. The reverse side of canvas will consist of separate single upright stitches. This stitch is used in many countries for covering large areas of canvas. It is found in Moroccan embroidery on designs similar to those of Assisi work, and in Yugoslavia to edge darning patterns on linen and fine canvas.

Montenegrin cross

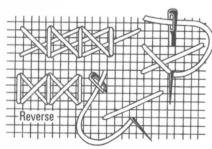

This is similar to long-armed cross but slightly more complex. It is a useful stitch, for the reverse of work is as attractive as the right side. Begin as for long-armed cross by taking a diagonal stitch 4 threads up and 8 vertical threads to the right. Bring needle back through 4 threads down and 4 threads to the left. Take a diagonal stitch 4 threads up and 4 threads to the left, bringing needle out at same point as before on the lower line. Then work an upright stitch across 4 horizontal threads. Continue in this way.

Oblong cross

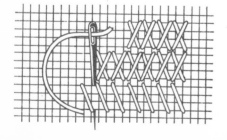

This is worked over 4 horizontal and 2 vertical threads to form a narrow upright cross. The first arm of the cross is worked in the first row, making the stitch from top left-hand corner down to bottom right-hand corner. On the return journey, the remaining arm is worked from bottom left-hand up to top right-hand corner. The exposed canvas between rows of oblong cross stitches can be filled in with back stitches, using a contrast or toning thread colour if wished. Back stitches may also be worked across the centre of the crosses.

Reversed cross

In this stitch, the basic cross stitch is alternated with straight cross stitches. Then a 2nd 'layer' of stitching is worked over these, usually in a finer and contrasting coloured thread— straight crosses are worked over the basic crosses, and basic crosses worked over straight crosses. Work in diagonal rows.

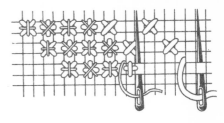

Smyrna or double cross

Also called Leviathan.

This consists of a basic cross stitch, with a straight cross over it, and is usually worked over 4 horizontal and 4 vertical threads. Work a basic cross as usual, then bring needle out on bottom line in centre of canvas threads. Take a straight upward stitch over 4 horizontal threads and complete as for straight cross stitch. Each complete Smyrna stitch should be completed before moving on to the next. By using a contrasting thread colour for alternate stitches, an attractive chequer pattern can be created.

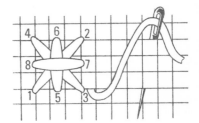

Straight or upright cross

In this the cross is worked with one horizontal straight stitch, and one vertical straight stitch, each over 2 threads of the canvas. Work vertical stitch first, then complete stitch with horizontal stitch before moving on to work the next stitch. In the 2nd row, work stitches between the stitches of the previous row so the rows interlock.

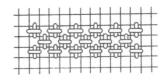

Two-sided Italian cross

This stitch has a similar appearance on the right and the wrong sides of canvas. It consists of a basic cross stitch bounded by straight stitches. The complete stitch may be worked in 2 journeys, or each stitch may be completed before moving to the next. It may be worked over 3 by 3 threads of the canvas, or fewer or more as required. Take first stitch from lower left-hand corner straight across 3 vertical threads (or number required) to the right. Bring needle out at starting point, then work a diagonal stitch 3 horizontal threads up, and 3 vertical threads to the right. Again bring needle out at starting point. Now work a straight vertical straight stitch from this point across 3 threads. Bring needle out 3 horizontal threads down and 3 vertical threads to the right and work a diagonal stitch 3 threads up and 3 vertical threads to the left across diagonal stitch previously worked. Continue in this way. Work 2nd row immediately below so each cross is bounded by 4 straight stitches (except in first and last

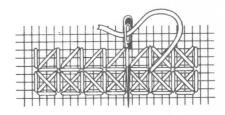

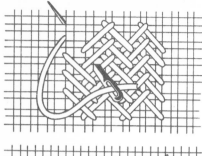

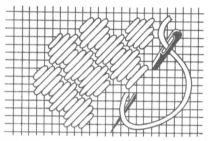

rows). To work this stitch in 2 journeys, on first journey (from left to right) work first 3 stitches in each complete stitch. On return journey (from right to left) complete the final diagonal of the cross.

CROSSING

This is worked from top to bottom, or bottom to top in diagonal rows. Diagonal stitches are taken over 4 horizontal threads and 4 vertical threads of the canvas. The direction of each row of stitches is alternated, and stitches are overlapped by 2 threads of the canvas.

DIAGONAL

As its name implies this consists of stitches worked diagonally across the canvas. Work from top left to bottom right of area to be covered. In its traditional form, each stitch is worked in turn over the intersections of the canvas threads as follows: over 2, 3, 4 and 3 intersections, then the sequence is repeated. Continue in this way to the end of the row. In the 2nd row the blocks of stitches fit into the zig-zag of previous row. As a variation on diagonal stitch a row of tent stitches (see page 61) can be worked between the zig-zag rows of diagonal stitches.

DIAMOND EYELET

This consists of 16 individual stitches. It is worked from the centre outwards. The first stitch is the top upright stitch which should be taken over 4 horizontal threads. Then working to the left, take stitches in turn over 3 horizontal threads and one vertical thread to the left, then over 2 horizontal threads and 2 vertical threads to the left, then over one horizontal thread and 3 vertical threads to the left, then a straight stitch over 4 vertical threads (this should be at right angles to the first stitch worked). Continue in this way round eyelet until diamond is complete. A row of back stitches may be worked round diamond if wished to hide the canvas. When using this stitch as a background, work in diagonal rows.

EYE

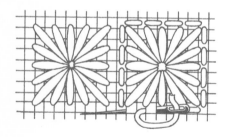

This, like the diamond eyelet, incorporates 16 individual stitches, but this time the eyelet is worked to form a square covering in total 8 horizontal and 8 vertical threads. Stitches are all worked from the centre outwards, leaving 2 threads of the canvas between each stitch. Begin with top upright stitch and work round to the left. When the eye is complete, finish with an outline of back stitches right round, working each back stitch over 2 threads of the canvas.

Note. This stitch may be worked over 4 by 4 threads only—it is usually then termed simply an *eyelet*.

FERN

This is worked from top to bottom. Bring needle through at top left-hand corner of area which stitching is to cover. Take a downward diagonal stitch 2 vertical threads to the right and 2 horizontal threads down. Bring needle through one vertical thread to the left then take an upward diagonal stitch 2 threads to the right, 2 threads up. Bring needle back out 3 threads to the left and one thread down. Continue in this way. Provided the canvas thread count is constant the number of threads covered by this stitch can be altered to suit the mesh of the canvas, and the need of the design for either a short, broad stitch or a long, narrow stitch. If necessary, work a line of back stitches between the vertical rows to give better coverage of canvas.

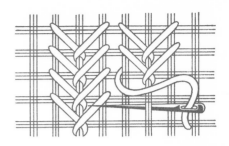

FILLINGS AND GROUNDINGS

These are solid areas of stitching normally used for the background of a design. They may be worked in any stitch, although some stitches obviously lend themselves to background work more readily than others. Only one colour may be used, or 2 or more contrasting or toning shades, if preferred. A few simple fillings are shown in the illustration below.

FISHBONE

This is worked over 3 horizontal and 3 vertical threads, each long diagonal stitch caught down with a short stitch across one thread. Rows are worked in a zig-zag alternating pattern. Begin by bringing needle out at left-hand side of work 3 threads down from top of area where stitching is to appear. Take a diagonal stitch upwards 3 vertical threads to the right and 3 horizontal threads up. Bring needle out one vertical thread to the left and take a short diagonal stitch across intersection of canvas threads. Bring needle out 3 horizontal threads down and 3 vertical threads to the left. Continue in this way. In the 2nd row, work stitches in alternate direction, working the row from bottom to top.

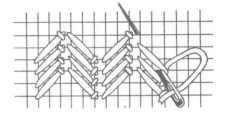

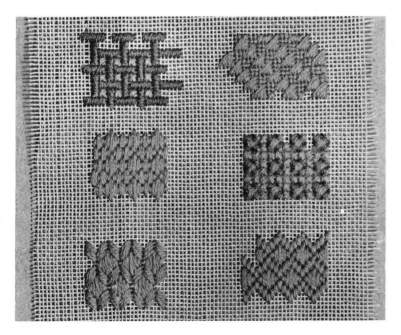

A selection of fillings.

51

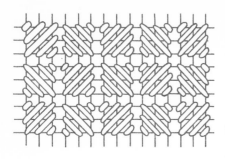

FLAT

This is worked in blocks of stitches in a similar way to mosaic stitch (see page 58) but the effect is entirely different, resembling a type of parquet flooring. Each complete block consists of 3 small diagonal stitches covering in total 2 horizontal threads and 2 vertical threads of the canvas, the first stitch covering one intersection of canvas threads, the 2nd covers 2 intersections, the 3rd covers one intersection. The next square of stitches is worked so the stitches slant in the opposite direction from the first square. Continue in this way.

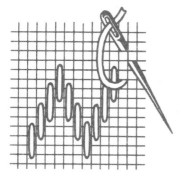

Flat stitch variation (see diagram above, left)

Work similar alternating blocks of stitches but this time cover 3 horizontal threads, 3 vertical threads. Each block will then consist of 5 stitches, covering in turn: one intersection, 2 intersections, 3 intersections, 2 intersections, one intersection.

FLORENTINE OR FLAME (see also page 79)

There are innumerable variations of this stitch, but in its simplest basic form, it consists of straight vertical stitches worked over 4 horizontal threads of the canvas. Stitches are stepped up or down 2 threads at a time to form zig-zags. The 2nd row is an exact repetition of the first, so stitches fit together. It is usual to work rows in graduated shades of one basic colour.

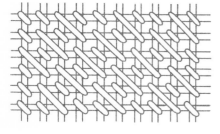

FLORENCE STITCH (diagonal Florentine)

This is worked in diagonal rows, in long and short diagonal stitches, worked alternately over one then 2 intersections of the canvas threads, or alternately over 2 then 4 intersections.

FRENCH

This is worked diagonally from top left to bottom right of area to be covered. It consists of a pair of upright stitches worked over 4 horizontal threads of the canvas and between 2 vertical threads. Each stitch in turn is caught down with a small horizontal central stitch—the left-hand stitch of the pair is tied down to the left-hand vertical thread of the canvas, and the right-hand stitch of the pair is tied down to the right-hand vertical thread of the canvas. To work the stitch, bring needle through at lower point of where stitch is to occur. Take a straight upward stitch over the 4 horizontal threads of the canvas, bring needle back out 2 horizontal threads below and to the left of the left-hand vertical thread. Take a small straight horizontal stitch across vertical stitch just worked and bring needle out in same mesh of canvas where first stitch began. Take another straight vertical stitch (still keep within the same pair of vertical threads) over 4 horizontal threads as before. Bring needle through 2 horizontal threads below and to the right of the right-hand vertical thread. Take a small horizontal stitch across vertical stitch just worked, from right to left, and insert needle between the 2 vertical stitches. Bring needle through 4 horizontal threads below and one vertical thread to the right, in readiness for the next stitch. Continue in this way.

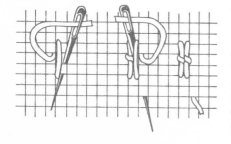

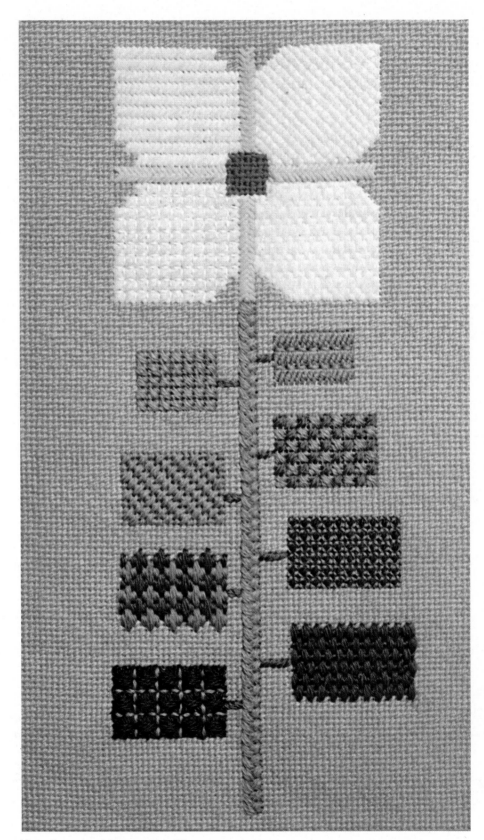

Your first sampler—see page 75.

Three modern tapestry embroidered pictures.
Right: Mrs. Siddons, a replica of an Old Master painting, working in half cross and tent stitches.
Below: Blaze.
Bottom of page: Pheasants. Penelope Designs O/M2, F/P504 and H476.

GOBELIN
Another important group of stitches with many variations.

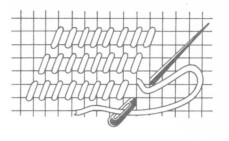

To work the basic gobelin stitch, sometimes known as oblique gobelin, work in horizontal rows from top to bottom of the area to be covered. Work first row from left to right. Bring needle through to right side of work. Take a diagonal stitch downwards across 2 horizontal threads and through to the wrong side, 1 vertical thread to the left. Bring needle out 2 horizontal threads up, and 2 vertical threads to the right. Continue in this way. The 2nd row is worked from right to left but this time the needle is inserted from above downwards instead of upwards from below, in order to maintain the same slant of the stitch. In this basic form, gobelin stitch resembles tent stitch (see page 61) but it is in fact a variant of satin stitch and was in use as early as the 13th century as a filling on linen.

Encroaching gobelin

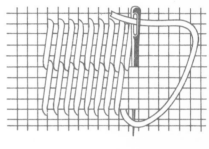

This is a longer stitch which passes across one vertical thread and covers 5 horizontal threads. Each row fits between the stitches of the previous row to give a very close fabric. As with the basic gobelin stitch, rows are worked alternately from left to right.

Plaited gobelin

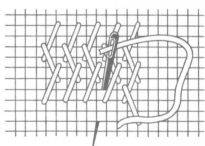

This is worked over 4 horizontal, 2 vertical threads of the canvas, the stitches overlapping the previous row to give a trellis effect. This is more open than any other variety of gobelin. Leave 2 vertical threads between each row and overlap the top part of each stitch across 2 threads of previous row. Alternate the slant of the stitches in each row to give a plaited effect.

Slanting gobelin
This is the basic gobelin stitch worked over 4 horizontal and 2 vertical threads, in rows as for the basic stitch.

Straight gobelin

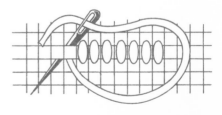

This consists of straight vertical stitches worked across 2 horizontal threads of the canvas. If wished (to give good canvas coverage) a tramming stitch can be worked first (see page 38) between the canvas threads then the straight stitches worked over the laid stitch. Straight gobelin most closely resembles the woven tapestry from which the stitch is named.

Wide gobelin

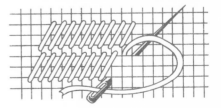

Work basic gobelin stitch over 3 horizontal and 2 vertical threads of the canvas.

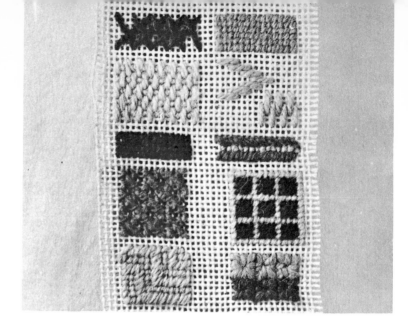

GREEK

This is worked in horizontal rows alternately from the left and From the right. Bring needle through below a horizontal thread of the canvas and to the left of a vertical thread. Take an upward diagonal stitch to the right across 2 intersections. Bring needle back out 2 vertical threads to the left. Take a downward diagonal stitch over 2 horizontal threads and 4 vertical threads to the right. Bring needle back through 2 vertical threads to the left. Continue in this way. At the end of the row bring needle through 2 horizontal threads below, and make first arm of the stitch (the short arm) diagonally across 2 intersections to the left. Continue as before, working stitch in reverse.

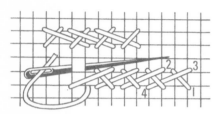

GROS POINT

See trammed tent stitch, page 62.

HUNGARIAN

This is a straight vertical stitch worked in horizontal rows in groups of 3 stitches over 2, 4 and 2 horizontal threads. A space of 2 vertical threads is left between groups so that the groups in the following row can be worked in the spaces to interlock. Contrast colours or threads can be effectively used for alternate rows.

Hungarian ground (point d'hongrie)

A variation of Hungarian stitch worked as a background filling. Rows of basic Florentine stitches are alternated with diamonds formed from 4 small upright stitches—each worked over 2 horizontal threads to fit into zig-zag of Florentine stitches. Each Florentine stitch is worked over 4 threads, stepped down 2 threads at a time, 3 stitches to each step.

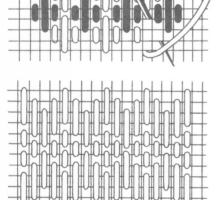

Hungarian stitch variation

Work in diamonds of straight vertical stitches: over 2 threads, 4 threads, 6 threads and 4 threads. The diamonds of 2nd row should fit between diamonds of first row to give a solid area of stitching.

JACQUARD

This should be worked over a fairly large area to show up to best advantage. It is worked diagonally in steps, from bottom right to top left of area to be covered, in alternate rows of tent stitches (see page 61) and long diagonal stitches taken over 2 vertical and 2 horizontal threads of the canvas, with 6 stitches to a step.

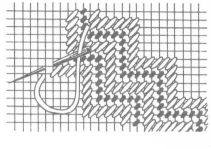

KELIM

This is a variation of knitting stitch (see below). It is worked in a similar way as knitting stitch, but rows are worked in horizontal lines over 4 vertical threads and 2 horizontal threads of the canvas.

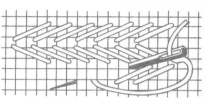

KNITTING STITCH (or tapestry stitch)

This gives the appearance of the right side of a stocking stitch pattern in knitting. It must be worked on double mesh canvas. It also is similar in appearance to chain stitch. Work right-hand side of chain first, starting at the bottom and working upwards. Bring needle through the centre of a vertical double thread, take a diagonal stitch upwards over 2 horizontal threads, and to the right of the vertical thread. Bring needle out below one horizontal thread and in centre of vertical thread. Continue in this way. When top of chain is reached, take needle round behind vertical thread and work from top to bottom working stitch in reverse as shown in diagram. Continue in this way.

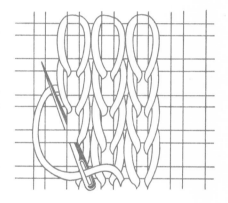

KNOTTED

This stitch covers the ground closely. One long diagonal stitch is worked over 3 (or 5) horizontal and 1 vertical threads, then a small stitch is worked over the centre intersection of canvas threads to tie the stitch down. Continue to work stitches in this way across row. In the following row, stitches are worked between stitches of previous row and overlapping by one thread.

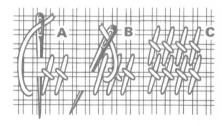

MILANESE

This is worked from right to left in diagonal rows of back stitch, in the first row stitches are worked alternately over one and 4 intersections of the canvas threads; in the 2nd row alternately over 2 and 3 intersections. In the 3rd row alternately over 3 and 2 intersections, and in the 4th row alternately over 4 and 1 intersections. Continue in this way. If wished, instead of starting a new thread for every row in order to work from right to left, work may be turned round for alternate rows so rows may be worked back and forth.

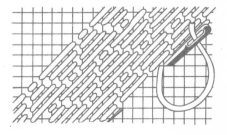

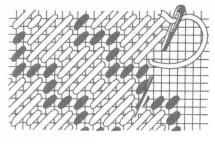
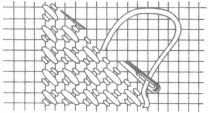

MOORISH

Diagonal rows of diagonal stitches worked across 2, 4 6 and 4 intersections of the canvas are alternated with stepped rows of tent stitch (see page 61), 3 stitches to a step. Again contrast threads or colours can be used for the alternating rows.

MOSAIC

Blocks of diagonal stitches are worked in a similar way to flat stitch (see page 52), but the direction of the stitches is constant. Blocks of 3 stitches covering 2 vertical and 2 horizontal threads of the canvas can be worked: stitches in turn are worked over 1, 2 and 1 intersections of the canvas. Or the stitch may be worked on a larger scale to cover a square of 3 horizontal and 3 vertical threads. Here 5 individual stitches are needed, each in turn being worked over 1, 2, 3, 2 and 1 intersections. Blocks of stitches are worked diagonally across the area to be covered.

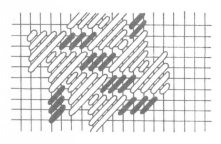

ORIENTAL

Work blocks of diagonal stitches, each block consisting of 4 stitches, worked in turn over 1, 2, 3 and 4 intersections of the canvas threads. Cover the canvas with diagonal rows of these 4-stitch triangles. Then fill in remaining spaces with gobelin stitches, each covering 2 horizontal threads and 2 vertical threads. Usually the gobelin stitches are worked in a contrasting colour to the triangles. The stitch should be worked over a large area to show to advantage.

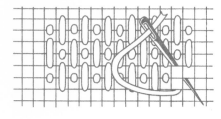

PARISIAN

This stitch makes a small close filling which is easily confused with Hungarian stitch. Upright straight stitches are worked alternately over 3 and 1 horizontal threads, the single-thread stitches placed midway between the 3-thread stitches. In the 2nd row, stitches are worked in alternate sequence from the first row to interlock and give a closely-covered fabric. Stitches may also be worked alternately over 4 and 2 threads. Stitches are worked in horizontal rows, so colour changes can only be in rows.

PETIT POINT

See tent stitch, page 61.

PLAIT

Also known as Spanish stitch.

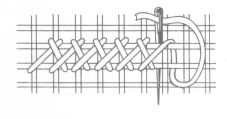

Stitches are worked to a depth of 2 horizontal threads. Bring needle out at left-hand side of lower line where stitching is to appear. Take an upward diagonal stitch across 2 horizontal threads and 2 vertical threads to the right. Bring needle through immediately below on lower line of stitching. Take a diagonal stitch upwards 2 horizontal threads up and 1 vertical thread to the left. Bring needle out immediately below on lower line of stitching. Continue in this way. Reverse side of work will consist of a number of straight vertical stitches.

PLAITED

This is worked in a similar way to fern stitch (see page 51) but rows which are worked downwards overlap each other by one vertical thread of the canvas. The result is a very closely interwoven fabric of stitching.

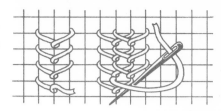

RAY

This can easily become bulky if the thread is too thick. Each complete stitch consists of 7 individual stitches; a total area of 3 horizontal threads and 3 vertical threads of the canvas is covered Work first row with individual stitches in each block all starting from top left-hand corner. Work 2nd row with stitches starting from top right-hand corner. The first individual stitch in each block is a straight horizontal stitch across 3 threads, the 4th stitch crosses diagonally to the opposite corner of square, and the 7th stitch is a straight vertical stitch over 3 threads. The 2nd and 3rd stitches are fitted between first and 4th, and the 5th and 6th stitches are fitted between 4th and 7th. Stitches may be worked in horizontal or vertical rows as wished.

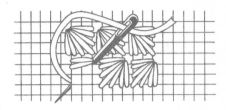

RENAISSANCE

This is worked vertically in groups of stitches. The first stitch is taken horizontally across 2 vertical threads of the canvas. Then 2 vertical straight stitches are worked taking each stitch over 2 horizontal threads, and across the stitch worked. The first vertical stitch will be at the left of the horizontal stitch, and the 2nd one in the centre. Take needle down behind 3 threads and repeat. Continue working groups of stitches below each other. When bottom of row is reached, work next row from bottom to top.

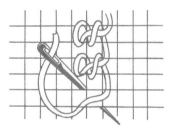

REP

Sometimes known as aubusson stitch.

This is always worked on double thread canvas. Tiny diagonal stitches are worked over the intersections of the canvas threads, always taking stitches over each complete vertical double thread, but over the individual horizontal threads. Work in horizontal rows.

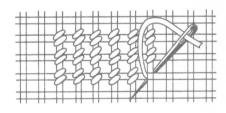

RICE

This is one of the most versatile of canvas stitches. Using a thick thread, work large basic cross stitches to cover 4 vertical and 4 horizontal threads of the canvas, then using a finer thread, in a contrasting colour if wished, work diagonal stitches over the corners of each cross. Work the big crosses first, then work the diagonal stitches back and forth in horizontal rows. This stitch can be worked on fine canvas using wool for the underlying cross stitch and stranded cotton for the corner threads, or at the other extreme it can be worked in thick wool on rug canvas for washable mats, in which case the tying down thread should be the same as the cross stitch thread. Various geometric patterns can be made by working blocks of stitches in different colours.

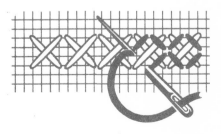

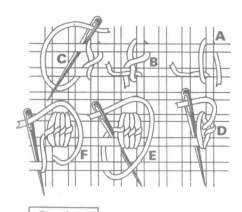

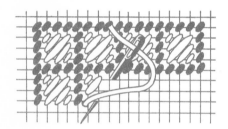

ROCOCO

This should be worked on a wide mesh canvas. Groups of stitches are set in alternate squares of the canvas mesh, leaving holes between. Work diagonally from top right down to bottom left of area to be covered. Each group consists of 4 upright stitches all worked over the same 2 horizontal threads and between same 2 vertical threads of the canvas. As each of the upright stitches is worked it is caught down in the centre with a small horizontal stitch. The diagram shows the stage-by-stage working of the stitch. The final 2 diagrams show how one group of stitches is completed and then the following one begun. It is important to choose the right thread so each group of stitches will completely fill the mesh of the canvas without being over-bulky. The diagram, left, shows the effect produced when a pattern of rococo stitches has been completed.

SATIN

This consists merely of single stitches worked either straight or diagonally over any number of canvas threads. The satin stitch sampler illustrated below shows a number of variations of this stitch. Some pieces of work—for instance, Norweave embroidery—are based entirely on blocks of satin stitch (see page 85).

SCOTTISH

This is an attractive stitch. Squares of diagonal stitches covering in turn 1, 2, 3, 2 and 1 intersections of the canvas threads, are outlined with tent stitches (see page 61) each covering a single intersection. All the diagonal stitches should slant in the same direction. As a variation to the basic pattern, 2 rows of tent stitches may be worked to separate the blocks of slanting stitches.

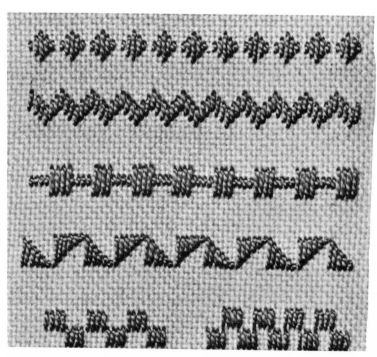

Sampler of satin stitch variations.

SHELL

Take 4 vertical straight stitches over 6 horizontal threads moving one vertical thread to the left for each stitch. After the 4th stitch, bring needle through between the centre pair of horizontal threads and between 2nd and 3rd vertical threads. Take a short horizontal stitch over one vertical thread, and over the 4 vertical stitches, thus drawing them together into a cluster. Bring needle out 3 horizontal threads down and 2 vertical to the left. Continue along row in this way. After row of clusters has been completed link them together by coiling thread twice into the horizontal stitches of adjoining clusters. Finally work back stitches between rows to cover canvas.

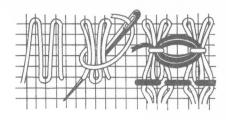

SMALL CHEQUER

This is a combination of mosaic stitch (see page 58) and tent stitch (see page 61). Blocks of mosaic stitches, covering 2 horizontal and 2 vertical threads of the canvas, each stitch in turn worked over 1, 2 then 1 intersections of the canvas, are alternated with groups of 4 tent stitches, worked over a similar area of canvas threads. It is best to work in diagonal rows, working all the blocks of mosaic stitches first, then returning to the beginning and filling in all the remaining areas with tent stitches. Two contrasting or toning colours may be used.

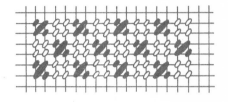

STAR

This is similar to Algerian eye stitch (see page 45) but only single stitches are worked instead of double. Each complete stitch consisting of 8 individual stitches is worked to cover an area of 4 horizontal and 4 vertical threads of the canvas. All stitches are worked into the central hole, beginning with top upright stitch and moving to the left for each subsequent stitch. Rows of star stitch are worked horizontally from left to right, or from right to left.

STEM

Vertical rows of diagonal stitches, each stitch is worked over 2 horizontal and 2 vertical threads of the canvas. The direction of each row of stitches is alternated. Back stitches can be worked between rows, if wished.

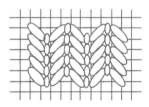

TENT

Another important stitch often used entirely on its own. It is the best stitch for very fine work, and can be useful for filling in areas where a larger stitch would spoil the line of the design, and a less squared shape is required. The term needlework tapestry is often applied to work done only in tent stitch as the finished appearance so closely resembles a woven tapestry. In the history of embroidery tent stitch can be traced at least as far back as the 13th century when it was used on the border of the Syon Cope (see page 6). More thread lies on the back than on the front of the canvas, which contributes to the hardwearing qualities of a tent stitch design. The term tent stitch is believed to be derived

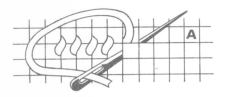

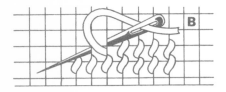

from the old word *tenture* or *tenter* (from *tendere*, to stretch) which was the name formerly given to the frame on which embroidery was stretched. The phrase 'to be on tenterhooks' comes from the same source. Tent stitch is really a sort of half cross stitch. Worked on single thread canvas it is sometimes called petit point. Worked on double thread canvas, over a tramming stitch (see page 38) it is known as gros point, or trammed tent stitch.

Each tent stitch consists of a diagonal stitch over one intersection of canvas threads. Trammed and untrammed tent stitches can be combined in the same piece of work by using double thread canvas, and opening up the threads of the double mesh for the untrammed stitches, and working them over single intersections of the threads.

Ideally tent stitch should be worked in diagonal rows as this prevents distortion of the canvas, and gives a good even coverage of canvas. For downward rows, take stitch from bottom to top diagonally then across one intersection then bring needle down vertically behind 2 horizontal threads. For upward rows take stitch from bottom to top as before but then take needle horizontally behind 2 vertical threads. Continue in this way.

When tent stitch has to be worked in horizontal rows, the rows can be worked from the left, or from the right. For rows from left to right, work each stitch from top to bottom then bring needle out one horizontal thread up and 2 vertical threads to the right. Repeat to the end of the row. For rows from right to left, work stitch from bottom to top and bring needle out one horizontal thread down, 2 vertical threads to the left. All stitches should slant in the same direction.

Reversed tent
This is worked in vertical lines, each stitch worked over 2 horizontal and one vertical thread. The direction of each row of stitches is alternated.

TRAMMING AND TRAMMED STITCHES
See page 38.

VELVET
This is basically a cross stitch plus a loop. After the first arm of the cross has been worked, repeat the stitch exactly, over the same intersection of canvas threads and allow a loop to form. Complete the cross stitch. The loop is then held in position by the cross stitch. Continue in this way across row. Afterwards the loops may be cut if wished to give a piled effect. In order to achieve an even row of loops, they can be worked over a knitting needle or any similar narrow rod.

WEB
This is a useful background stitch which must be worked on double thread canvas. Working in diagonal rows, thread is laid diagonally across whole area to be filled then the thread is tied down with small stitches taken between mesh of double thread of canvas. The small stitches are worked in alternate sequence to previous row to give the effect of a closely-woven fabric.

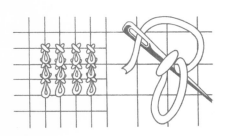

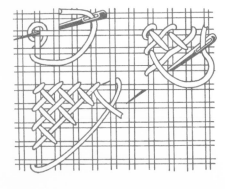

finishing touches

In whatever way you plan to use your canvas embroidery—as a wall hanging or picture, a cushion, stool top, kneeler, handbag or any other of the many popular and suitable ways in which this embroidery can be displayed—when the actual stitching is complete, before the design can be made up into its finished form, it is important to check your canvas carefully to see if it has been pulled out of shape by the stitching. Even when correctly mounted on a frame, the stitches can still distort the canvas.

If you have not used a frame, and you are satisfied there is no distortion to the canvas, all that will be necessary is to press the work carefully, on a soft pad so as not to flatten it on the wrong side with a hot iron over a damp cloth. Leave to dry before making up into finished form. If you have worked on a frame, and there is little or no distortion to the canvas, press it in the following way: keeping the embroidery still securely fixed in its frame (tighten strings if necessary), lay it right side down on a flat clean surface. Using a damp sponge, thoroughly dampen the back of the embroidery. Leave until completely dry—usually a minimum of twenty-four hours is required for this drying process—then remove work from the frame.

When removing work from a frame, snip through the stitching at top and bottom which was used to attach canvas to webbing of frame. Then snip through lacing down the sides and carefully lift canvas clear of frame. It is essential to keep the unworked 2–3in. border round embroidery as this facilitates the mounting of work into its finished form.

STRETCHING THE CANVAS

If canvas has been badly distorted, it will be necessary to stretch it before making up or mounting. Do this as follows:

1 Cover a firm board or wooden surface (a good-sized pastry board is ideal), slightly larger than the completed piece of canvas, with 2 or 3 sheets of blotting paper.

2 Thoroughly dampen the blotting paper.

3 If the work is badly distorted, dampen the back of the canvas with a sponge soaked in cold water. Apply sponge with a dabbing action; do not ever rub. Make sure the entire area of canvas, including unworked border, is evenly dampened. This soaking will loosen the gum or stiffening agent in the canvas, so making the canvas pliable, and able to be pulled into the required size and shape.

4 Place the work right side up on the board over the blotting paper and start to pin along one side at intervals of 1in., parallel with the side of the board. If it is a heavy piece of work, use small nails instead of drawing pins. Do not pin into the embroidery itself; only into the unworked border.

Above: a dramatic modern canvas work picture, in which a three-dimensional pattern in white is superimposed against a red, orange and black background. Worked mainly in tent and satin stitches.
Below: stretching canvas.

5 Working on the opposite edge, pull taut and pin, after making sure that the corners are true and the grain of the canvas straight. This edge must also run parallel to the edge of the board. When these two sides are secured, continue pinning the other two sides again inserting pins at 1in. intervals.

6 When you are satisfied the canvas has been adequately stretched leave in this position until the canvas is thoroughly dry: this can take up to two or three weeks. As the gum or stiffening agent in the canvas dries it resets the canvas threads into the new shape, so giving a permanently flat and even piece of work.

7 When the canvas is completely dry, carefully remove pins. If the canvas has been very badly pulled out of shape it may be necessary to repeat the stretching process.

MOUNTING

If you intend to use your embroidery as a picture or wall hanging, before framing you will have to mount the canvas on a suitable sheet of cardboard, or hardboard, if large.

1 First of all cut a piece of cardboard to the size of the actual embroidery (i.e. excluding the unworked border). Place embroidery wrong side down centrally on the cardboard. Stretching the canvas tautly and evenly, fold the unworked border on to the wrong side of cardboard. Fold the top edge over first, and secure with pins into edge of cardboard. Then fold bottom edge over and secure with pins in a similar way. Finally fold over and pin the side edges.

2 Now, using strong thread, secure these folded-over edges by lacing the top and bottom edges together, and the two side edges. For each lacing begin at the midway point and work outwards at either side.

3 Before putting your backed embroidery into a picture frame, it must first be set on to a mounting board. Mounting board is a sort of stiff card, and is available from art supply and photographic shops in a good range of colours: choose a colour which will harmonise with your embroidery.

4 The cardboard-backed canvas is placed on a sheet of mounting board, which should be larger all round than the cardboard-backed canvas (the exact measurement will depend on the size of your work). Canvas should be placed on mounting board so the spaces above it and at each side are equal. The space below the window should be slightly deeper.

5 Another sheet of mounting board is secured on front of work, with the central area cut out to form a 'window' for your embroidery. This should overlap the edges of the embroidery slightly. Cut mounting board with a razor knife (not scissors), taking care to cut window frame section evenly and accurately.

6 Place window sheet right side down on a clean flat surface. Place embroidery also right side down centrally on the window frame sheet. Secure edges of embroidery to frame with strips of self-adhesive transparent tape.

7 Now carefully spread wrong side of backing sheet of mounting board with a thin layer of fabric glue and very carefully place

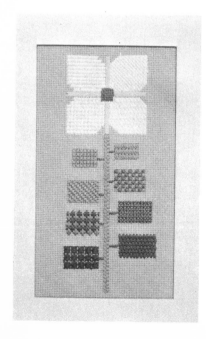

A stool can have gimp tacked round edge of canvas covered pad. Design is worked in tent stitch.

this on top of embroidery and window frame. Make sure the edges align exactly then press firmly together. Leave to set over-night preferably weighted with books or other heavy objects. If wished, set mounted work into a picture frame.

MAKING UP YOUR EMBROIDERY
Hassocks and kneelers
See page 86.

Stools
All types of stool (except those where the embroidery is fitted over a pad and slotted into a stool frame) need to have quantity of canvas assessed carefully before beginning work. Normally the patterned area will appear on the top of the stool only, but sufficient background area must be worked to provide side drops—sometimes a repeat of the pattern motif, or a part of it, is included on the side drop.

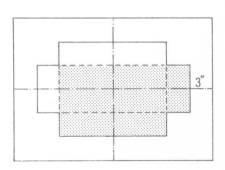

When assessing total quantity of canvas required, take a total horizontal measurement to include side drops, and a total vertical measurement also to include side drops. Add about 3in. to this measurement all round for the unworked border area.

When you mark out your canvas prior to framing-up, mark out with tacking stitches the central area of stool, and then mark the side drops all round (see diagram, right). Embroidery is worked only within these lines—i.e. there will be four corner areas of unworked canvas. If you are working from a pattern chart, often the chart will only show one short side drop and one long side drop. You must remember to add the two remaining side drops to correspond.

After the embroidery is complete, and the canvas has been stretched, stitch corner edges together, right sides facing. Stitch close to the finished embroidery, using a neat backstitch seam. No canvas should show on the right side of work when corners are turned to the right side.

Trim excess canvas away from corner, and trim the unworked canvas border to 1½in. from embroidery. Turn this border to wrong side of work, pressing corner areas to one side, and herringbone stitch neatly in place. Turn cover to right side and fit over stool.

Secure cover to stool with upholstery tacks nailed at intervals all round lower edge of cover. Smooth the cover evenly into position as you work. Start tacking at the midway point of each side and work outwards.

Cushions

As a rule, a canvas work cushion has the embroidery on one face of the cushion only. The other side of the cushion is made from a matching or toning suitable furnishing fabric. Interesting and attractive effects can be achieved by a subtle and clever choice of fabric—for instance, by matching exactly just one particular shade in the embroidery; by matching texture of fabric to embroidery stitches.

The fabric should however be of similar weight to the canvas— i.e. do not have a piece of heavy-weight canvas worked in rug wools backed with flimsy silk. And unless the embroidery was a particularly plain all-over design, it would be unwise to try to combine a patterned fabric with a canvas embroidery. An important design point to bear in mind when plotting your own pattern for a canvas work cushion is that the design should be acceptable from any angle, even upside-down—for cushions do not stay the same way up all the time! There should in fact be no 'upside-down' to the design.

The principle of making up a cushion, whether square, round, oblong or any other shape, is virtually the same: a cushion pad will be required which should measure approximately ½in. less round all edges than the finished cushion, so that the embroidered cover can slip on and off easily.

Below: two sides of the same cushion. A vivid modern design worked in rice stitch and cross stitch.

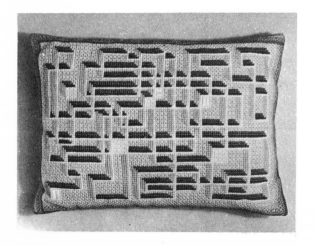

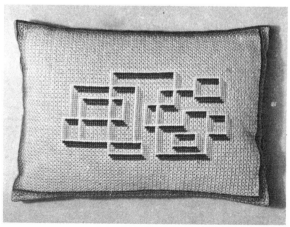

After canvas embroidery is complete, and canvas has been stretched, trim away excess canvas to within 1in of the embroidery. Cut a piece of furnishing fabric for the other side of the cushion to the same size as your trimmed canvas.

Place canvas and material together, right sides facing, and stitch round three sides, taking 1in. turnings. Use a strong thread and take neat even back stitches close to the finished embroidery but not overlapping it. When cushion is turned right side out there should be no unworked canvas showing.

When the three sides are sewn together, turn cover right side out. Insert pad, turn in seam allowance along remaining side and neatly oversew edges together. Alternately the edges can be fastened with press studs, or with self-adhesive nylon fastening. If wished, a cord trimming can be added round the edges of the cushion.

Bags
A bag may be made wholly from a piece of canvas embroidery, or it may have a panel of canvas work inserted into it.

To make a bag wholly from canvas work, when embroidery is complete and canvas has been stretched, trim canvas to within 1in of embroidery then use this as a pattern to cut a piece of interlining and a piece of lining fabric.

Individual making-up instructions will vary according to style of bag but in general the principle is to stitch embroidery side seams and base seam, if required, so the embroidery is in the shape of the finished bag. Make up the interlining in a similar way then insert into bag, wrong sides together, turn in seam allowance along remaining edges of canvas on to interlining and stitch lightly to hold in place.

Make up lining in a similar way, and insert into bag, wrong side against interlining. Turn in seam allowance along remaining top edge, and slip stitch neatly to canvas to hold in place.

To make an inset panel of canvas work, choose a strong hardwearing fabric suitable for this style of bag: a heavyweight linen is ideal. On the section of bag where you wish inset panel to appear, mark out on the wrong side of fabric the exact area of embroidered panel. Cut out this area, cutting $\frac{1}{2}$in. inside the marked line to allow for seam allowance.

Above: two canvas work handbags, one a modern design in a variety of stitches, the other a traditional design in tent stitch.

Left: a bag with an inset of canvas embroidery (see also page 165).

Place embroidered panel centrally in the cut-out 'window', placing right side of embroidery against wrong side of fabric. Tack in place exactly along seam allowance line. Clip fabric at corners into this line. Working on the right side, turn in the hem along each edge, and stabstitch securely in place to canvas.

Make up bag, lining and interlining in style required.

Chair seats and stools and inset pads
Embroidery should be worked to fit size of chair or stool pad exactly. When embroidery is complete and canvas has been stretched, place embroidery centrally over the chair or stool pad, fold borders of unworked canvas to the wrong side of pad, and secure firmly with a row of upholstery tacks on the underside.

AFTER-CARE OF CANVAS EMBROIDERY
Although the yarns and threads used to work canvas embroidery are often washable, canvas rarely is. Submerging in water would soften the threads of the canvas and in all probability spoil it completely. A piece of canvas work must therefore always be dry cleaned. It is advisable never to let an embroidery become too dirty before cleaning: providing dry cleaning is carried out carefully, no matter how frequently it is done, no possible harm can come to the embroidery.

You can however freshen up your embroidery between proper cleanings with an application of a good proprietary brand of aerosol dry-cleaner.

After cleaning it may be necessary to restretch the canvas back into shape. Even if the shape of the piece appears to have been retained, a stretching will improve it, revive it and give the embroidery renewed flatness.

Above and below: stools with inset pads covered with traditional tent stitch embroidery.

transferring designs to canvas

There are several possible methods of transferring a pre-determined design on to your canvas.

If you are using a needlework tapestry kit, this normally comes complete with prepared canvas, all threads necessary for working the design, and complete making instructions. The canvas will usually have the design 'painted' on to it. You simply follow the painted design, using thread colours to match the 'painting' and covering the areas of canvas indicated. These kits offer a wide variety of subject matter from traditional floral designs to facsimiles of old master paintings. It is even possible to buy kits for making your own canvas embroidery greetings cards.

PAINTING YOUR OWN DESIGN

If you are designing your own canvas embroidery, it is possible to paint your required design on to the canvas in a similar way to the bought kits. First plan your design roughly on a sheet of paper. When you are satisfied that you know what you want, and the relative balance and colours of your design, then paint on the design to your canvas, using a fine, good-quality paintbrush and waterproof Indian ink. This should be done after preparing canvas but before framing-up.

Alternatively, and for a more accurate transposition from paper to canvas, plan and draw out your design carefully on paper to the actual size of the canvas. Draw the design with a

Primitive, a modern tapestry embroidered picture; Penelope Design H490.

fairly heavy dark line—again, Indian ink is ideal. Then place the paper with the drawn design beneath the prepared canvas. Make sure paper is exactly in position, its centre lines matching centre lines of the canvas. The dark outline of the design should show through.

Again using a fine paintbrush and waterproof Indian ink, trace the design on to the canvas, following the outline showing through. Black is usually best but if work is to be in light colours a lighter ink can be used.

Although both these 'painting' methods give a clear design outline to follow, you will of course have to work out beforehand which stitches to use in which part of the work. Even if you prefer to evolve your design as you go along—as many experienced designers do—a certain amount of preliminary preparation will help to avoid mistakes, and subsequent wastage of time, canvas, thread and effort!

WORKING FROM A CHART

Another popular method of plotting a design is in chart form, on a squared graph. Each square on the graph, whatever its scale, represents one hole or thread of the canvas mesh. Different stitch types can be coded on the graph chart by means of different symbols.

If you are working a complicated design with a number of

Two quick tapestries, worked on canvas with 5 holes to the inch.
Above: Butterfly.
Left: Bird. Penelope Designs RO7 and RO5.

Two canvas embroidered pictures, each using a variety of stitches.
Right: cockerel design.
Below: owl picture (see page 146 for making instructions).

different stitches and thread colours, two diagrams may be necessary to give a clear guide to working: one diagram will be the squared chart which should be followed for position of stitches; the second diagram will show a replica of the design, this time on a plain background, and it will be keyed (with numbers or letters) to give a guide to stitches and colours used throughout the design (for example, see design illustrated on page 77).

Stitches such as Florentine, which cover several squares or holes of the canvas at once, are usually represented on the squared chart by a single line across the required number of squares.

This method gives a completely accurate version of the design, but it does necessitate a certain amount of laborious counting. The easiest way to cope with the counting is to mark off the graph in tens or eights—depending on the grid of the particular graph being used—then in a similar way, mark your canvas into groups of ten or eight with basting stitches (see page 33 for a fuller description of this marking technique).

Alternatively, if the grid of your graph paper is the same size as your canvas mesh, then the graph may simply be placed under the canvas, and the design traced off on to the canvas. If it is not wished to trace off the whole design, key points only could be transferred, to give a further guideline while work progresses.

ADAPTING A DESIGN

Although it is more usual to plot a design straight on to graph paper, sometimes you may come across a motif or design idea which you think could be translated into a canvas embroidery. The easiest way to transfer the design to your graph paper is first to take a tracing of the motif on thin tracing paper, then lay this traced drawing on top of your graph paper. The grid lines of the graph should show clearly through, thus giving you the necessary area for your design. Secure tracing paper to graph paper with pins or transparent self-adhesive tape. As no true curves can be produced in canvas work, where curved areas occur in the design they will have to be translated into a series of 'stepped' squares.

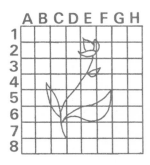

If you want to enlarge or reduce a design motif, take a tracing of the motif as described above, then draw a rectangle round the motif, close to its edges. Now divide this area first in half lengthways, and then in half crossways.

Subdivide these areas again. If the design is very big, it may be necessary to make further subdivisions to each section. Continue to subdivide until you feel each square contains a reasonably simplified area of the design.

Now draw out a similar squared area on a blank sheet of paper to the size required of amended motif. Square by square copy the design in the original drawing on to the squares of the new diagram, being careful to follow shapes and positions as accurately as possible. When you are satisfied the design is accurate, draw over it with Indian ink, and transfer to your canvas by painting method (see page 69).

Sometimes it is wished to keep the depth of a design, but to widen or reduce the width. In this case vertical lines are drawn at equal intervals across a section of the design, and through key

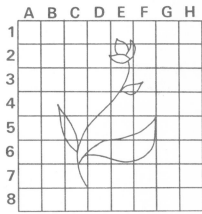

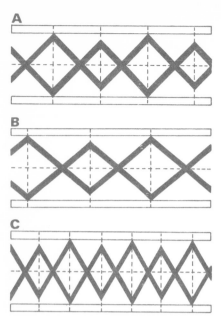

A

B

C

points. For instance, if the design consists of a series of repeated motifs, then vertical lines would be drawn through the same point of each repeat of the design.

Draw out a grid for the required new size of design. The depth will be the same as before, but the total width will be either increased or decreased, as required. Within this area, draw vertical lines at regular intervals, spacing them out to give the new motif width wished. Now draw in the design placing the key points of the repeated motifs on the vertical lines as before, and expanding or reducing the outline of the design between the key points as necessary.

The three diagrams, left, show how the same design can be widened and reduced. Diagram A shows the design in its original form; diagram B shows it widened; diagram C shows it reduced.

If you are working out your own design, and want to include a number of repeated shapes, the easiest way to maintain consistency in the repeats is to cut out a template of the shape in card and draw round this for each motif.

It is possible to use a template method directly on to your prepared canvas—simply lay the card shapes in position on the canvas, and paint round them with a fine paintbrush and waterproof Indian ink.

Canvas embroidered picture in· tent stitch, worked on a very fine mesh canvas.

your first sampler

After experimenting with threads, canvases and stitches, you should now be ready to embark upon a finished piece of work. A sampler is the traditional and ideal method for displaying the techniques and stitches you have so far learned. But as well as being a valuable 'reference book' of ideas, a sampler should too be an attractive piece of work, something you will be proud and pleased to hang up in your home for other people to see and admire.

Here is a first sampler for you to make which answers all requirements: it includes a varied selection of stitches and textures, but it makes a pleasant and eyecatching picture as well.

Follow the step-by-step instructions below for making up your sampler. Once you have successfully completed this design, you can move on to the patterns in the designs to make chapter beginning on page 102.

PREPARING THE CANVAS

White single thread canvas should be used for your sampler, with 12 threads to the inch. The finished sampler measures approximately 5in. wide by 10in. long, so cut a piece of canvas measuring 11in. by 16in. (to allow for an unworked border of 3in. all round).

The design runs lengthwise, so make sure you cut your canvas the right way up—the selvedges must run vertically. As soon as you have cut the strip, overcast the edges to prevent them from unravelling.

Now measure the centre point horizontally and vertically, as described on page 33, and mark these centres with basting. Mark out the total area the embroidery will cover.

The design uses a number of diagonal stitches, so it is recommended that the canvas is mounted on a frame for working the embroidery. Prepare the canvas and frame-up as described on pages 33 and 34. As this is a reasonably small piece of work a small frame with 12in. webbing will be quite adequate, and less cumbersome for working with than the bigger frames.

THREADS AND COLOURS

Once your canvas is prepared, select the threads you will use, and the right needle. The design uses a combination of double crêpe knitting wool, double knitting nylon yarn and crewel wool.
For the background: 1oz. double crêpe knitting wool in pink.
For the flower: 1oz. of double knitting nylon yarn in white; oddments in pale blue and tan.
For the leaves and stem: 1 skein each crewel wool in light, medium and dark green.
You will need a tapestry needle No. 17.

DIAGRAMS

The colour illustration on page 53 shows the finished sampler in just a little under its actual size. The diagram A shows the design marked out on a graph. The background lines on the graph represent the threads of your canvas. The blank arrows mark the centre points and these should coincide with your lines of basting stitches.

The positions of the various stitches are indicated on this diagram, each stitch represented by a different symbol. Although the symbols are often given on the holes of the graph, in every case the actual stitch is worked over the adjoining line or lines (representing threads of the canvas) depending on the stitch and the number of canvas threads it covers. Once you begin work you will find it a fairly simple matter to translate the design from the graph on to your canvas. You can, if you prefer, transfer the design on to your canvas by any of the methods explained on pages 69–73.

Diagram B gives a guide to the various thread colours used throughout the design. Once you have identified which stitch is being used in a particular part of the sampler, then establish which thread colour and type it is to be worked in, following this diagram and the colour key given below.

STITCH KEY (Diagram A)

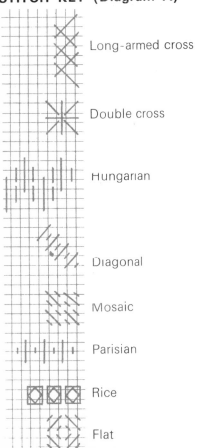

Long-armed cross

Double cross

Hungarian

Diagonal

Mosaic

Parisian

Rice

Flat

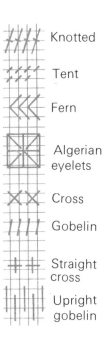

Knotted

Tent

Fern

Algerian eyelets

Cross

Gobelin

Straight cross

Upright gobelin

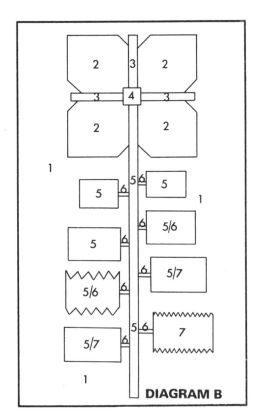

DIAGRAM B

COLOUR KEY (Diagram B)
1 Pink
2 White
3 Pale blue
4 Tan
5 Light green
6 Medium green
7 Dark green

76

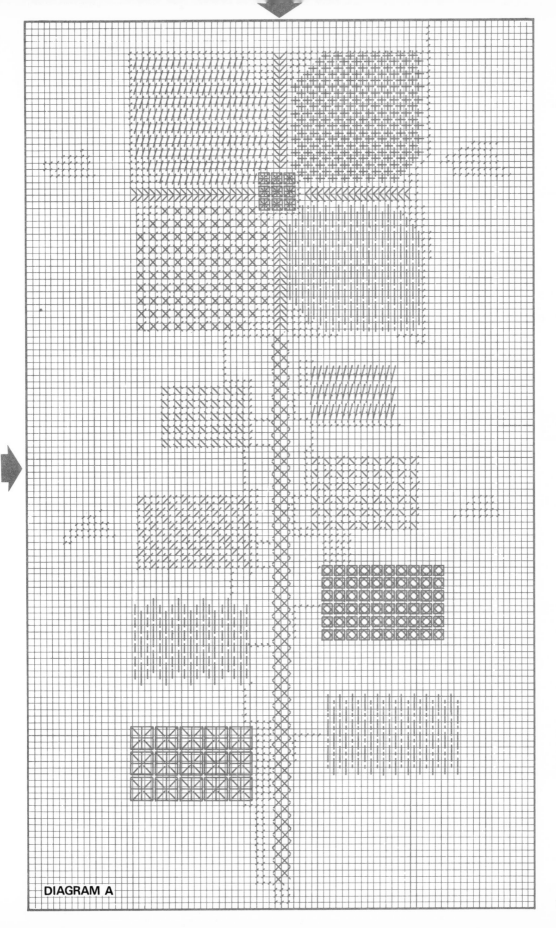

DIAGRAM A

Pomposa, tapestry bell pull; Penelope Design RO4.

STARTING WORK

Begin working the embroidery by stitching the main stem in longarmed cross stitch in light green. This is worked over the central 3 threads of your canvas.

Now work the leaves, starting at the bottom left and moving upwards, working each block of stitches within area indicated on diagram A, as follows:

1. Double cross stitch in dark green, with back stitches worked between rows, in light green.
2. Hungarian stitch, worked in alternate rows of light and medium green.
3. Diagonal stitch, in light green.
4. Mosaic stitch, in light green.

In a similar way, work leaves from bottom right upwards as follows:

1. Parisian stitch, in dark green.
2. Rice stitch, with basic cross in dark green, crossed corner stitches in light green.
3. Flat stitch, in alternate blocks of light and medium green.
4. Knotted stitch, with back stitches worked between rows, in light green.

Link each leaf to the main stem with a row of tent stitches in medium green.

The blue stamens on the flower are worked next, in fern stitch over 3 threads. Then work the centre of the flower in Algerian eyelets, with a single row of tent stitch on the right and lower sides, all in tan.

Now work the 4 petals of the flower, from lower left in a clockwise direction in white as follows:

1. Cross stitch, with back stitches worked between stitches and rows.
2. Gobelin stitch.
3. Straight cross stitch.
4. Upright gobelin stitch.

The background is worked entirely in tent stitch in pink. Work in diagonal rows to prevent distortion of the canvas, and to give practise in keeping an even tension. Cover area marked out on your canvas with background stitching.

TO FINISH OFF YOUR SAMPLER

When the embroidery is complete, canvas should be stretched as described on page 63. When you are satisfied canvas is adequately stretched, and completely dry, mount it on cardboard and mounting board, as described on page 64.

traditional techniques

FLORENTINE WORK

Florentine work, sometimes known as fianna or flame stitch because of the characteristic flame-like points of the traditional Florentine patterns, is a form of embroidery on canvas or any evenweave material which is worked with vertical stitches arranged in zig-zig lines.

Usually several different colours of thread are used, in graduated shades. It is a good and satisfying technique for a beginner to try because as the stitches are all straight there is no distortion of the canvas, and it is unnecessary even to use a frame.

The origin of Florentine work is uncertain, but it is believed to have been brought to Italy by a Hungarian who married one of the Medici family in the 15th century. It was particularly popular in England during the 16th century and again in the reign of Queen Anne. Many beautiful examples can be seen in old church hangings in Italy today. A set of chairs in the Bargello Museum, in Florence, have their seats embroidered in Florentine style—sometimes the technique is called Bargello work after these chairs.

Originally the work was used to cover entire surfaces including stool tops and chair seats, to add richness of texture and colour to the upholstery. And similarly today a canvas design in Florentine work should be rich and the canvas base well covered. Silk, wool and cotton are all suitable threads to use, provided they are thick enough to cover the canvas completely.

The embroidery can however also be worked on evenweave linen, where areas of unworked linen are contrasted against stitched areas. The colour of the material should be chosen to complement the colour of threads used to work the design. And the stitched areas should be closely filled as a thin thread would weaken the appearance of the design.

Traditionally a design uses several shades of the same colour arranged in bands or other shapes to give an attractive graduation of colour. However interesting work can be done by combining entirely different colours in the one piece of work but this is not the traditional form of the style.

Stitches are worked perpendicularly across a number of threads of the canvas (from two to six threads), stitches are varied in height and 'stepped' to create a waved pattern. The working instructions for the stitch are given on page 52.

The simplest Florentine design progresses across the canvas in a continuous zig-zag line with each stitch being taken over four horizontal threads of the canvas, and being stepped two horizontal threads above or below the last. For instance, start by stepping each stitch down two threads from the previous one until the lower level of zig-zag required is reached then step the stitches back up two threads at a time until the height of the zig-zag is reached. Continue in this way across work. The next line will be an exact repetition of the first but worked immediately below.

Variations of the basic zig-zag are almost limitless. Alterations in the length of stitch, number of stitches in each step, and in the step itself can change a simple zig-zag into a curve or scallop. When the curve is turned upside down, circular patterns result.

It is best always to start the first row of a piece of Florentine work in the centre and work outwards on either side. As Florentine stitch is an upright stitch, a thicker thread is needed to give good coverage to the canvas.

After mastering the technique with traditional threads, try experiments with unusual and novelty threads such as plastic raffia (see illustration, page 18).

The term Florentine really covers embroidery in four distinct styles:

1. Designs worked in Florentine stitch in the basic 4/2 step, as described above, or in a 6/3 step.

2. Floral designs worked in Hungarian ground (see page 56) with some other stitches. This style combines the characteristic shading with floral designs worked in Hungarian ground. The Hungarian ground produces a subsidiary pattern distinct from the colour pattern which adds an unexpected texture to the surface but can be confusing to the worker, even after some experience.

In historical examples, errors in working are frequent enough to suppose that the effort to shade flowers and at the same time follow the intricacies of Hungarian ground counting proved too much for many embroiderers. Probably far more of this style still exists in Italy than at present has come to light, certainly much was done judging by the number of fragments in museums.

A perfect example of the style is preserved at Drayton House, England, where the 11ft. high state bed has a complete set of curtains, cornice, top and mattress valances worked in wool and a little silk, made between 1660 and 1680. The design reflects French taste and Dutch flower painting and many flowers are recognisable. This style was used in hangings made in 17th century Italy, and on upholstery in 18th century England.

3. Flame patterns (i.e. graduated ranges of colours from light to dark, using five or six shades), in Florentine stitch, generally in the 4/2 step.

4. Flame patterns worked in Hungarian ground.

Even Florentine stitch worked in the basic 4/2 step can follow a quite complicated line, if care is taken to plot out a pattern beforehand on graph paper. A magnificent example of Hungarian ground flame stitch can be seen at Parham, Sussex, England, where the Great Bed still has its complete set of hangings worked in many soft shades of brown, gold and pink. Other sets of hangings at Deerfield, Mass., also show that this stitch can be very attractive. These curtains, however, lack the elegance of those at Parham, where tone and proportion as well as detailed attention to the edges of all the valances and the tiny embroidered band which covers every seam, combine in making a significant work of art.

Cushion cover from the Greek islands worked in cross stitch; 17th century.

Today small articles can be decorated successfully with Florentine embroidery if fine canvas—20 or 24 threads to the inch—and stranded cotton are used: napkin rings, pen and pencil cases, slippers, mules and small bags. Cushions, loose seat pads, stool tops and hassocks are better worked in wool on slightly coarser canvas. Glenshee and willow fabric are excellent for place mats, tray and tablecloths, aprons and cushions when the whole ground is not covered. Borders with corners and central square designs can be worked out with the help of a mirror (see page 100).

When a Florentine pattern has been carried out usually there are spaces left at the edges of the canvas. These should be filled in afterwards with any neat form of straight stitch.

CROSS STITCH

Cross stitch covers another vast area of embroidery, and belongs to the class of stitches which come from following, as it is only natural to do, the mesh of a coarse linen, net, open web or canvas upon which the work is done. A stitch inevitably bears some relation to the material on which it is worked, but canvas or coarse linen almost compels a stich based upon the cross lines of its mesh.

For this reason, cross stitch is one of the oldest of all stitches; it is simple, effective and can stand on its own satisfactorily without the addition of other stitches. The technique of cross stitch has early beginnings and was found in the peasant embroideries of many European countries. Through the centuries it has been used extensively on all household articles—bedcovers, pillows, cushions and tablecloths.

Many peasant designs are so strongly constructed that they

would not lose their impact if worked only in black on white. The secret of much of the success lies in the arrangement of stitches in blocks, so shaped that they in turn make shapes of the background spaces, and so give a dual pattern.

As with Florentine embroidery, cross stitch can be worked on a canvas base, and forms the basis for an important group of canvas stitches, or it can be worked in an evenweave linen. If you wish to work cross stitch embroidery on a fine fabric, then a piece of canvas can be pinned over the material, and stitches worked over this. Afterwards the threads of the canvas are pulled away to reveal the worked design on the fabric (see page 101 for fuller instructions for working over canvas in this way).

The technique of cross stitch has long been popular for working monograms and lettering of all kinds—a cross stitch sampler was a popular item of needlework in Victorian days.

Cross stitch at its most beautiful can be seen on peasant costume of Slavonic countries. Each has its own traditional designs and colours, shown to perfection on snow white linen. By contrast, the proliferation of work done in Victorian England, charming though it is, sometimes seems insipid and lacking in any true artistic worth.

A women's magazine published at the end of the 19th century in Victorian England writes enthusiastically of the 'beauty of modern cross stitch' thus:

'Cross stitch has ever proved such a valuable friend to devotees of needlecraft that it is small matter for surprise to find it frequently used for the embellishment of the pastrons, revers, panels, straps and bands that form such indispensable features of present-day costumes.'

The same article went on to advise: 'Cross stitch is moreover an ideal method for ornamenting the studiously simple yet dainty frocks and tunics in which sensible modern mothers are tastefully clothing their small children and younger daughters.'

Cross stitch has a large family of variations (see pages 47 to 50). Long-armed cross stitch is an important variation as it is used a great deal in stitched rugmaking. It forms a good edge when worked over the folded edges of the rug canvas. It is also useful for working over a join or fold such as when the top of a kneeler is joined to the gusset, and for the corners. When it is covering a fold, two rows of canvas must be left in the design over which to work it.

ASSISI WORK

This is another traditional form of counted thread embroidery, closely related to cross stitch. It takes its name from modern embroideries made in Assisi, in Italy. The earliest examples, which date from the 16th century, were not then known by the present name.

In its traditional form, it is worked on an ivory linen in blue or red, or occasionally green, with black. Patterns are based on stylised birds, animals, flowers and geometrical outline shapes. The design is first outlined in black with Holbein or double running stitch, then the background is blocked in with cross stitch or sometimes long-armed cross stitch, worked in blue or in red. Thus the background of the fabric is left unworked to form the design shapes.

Above: Assisi work in traditional style. Left: a modern Assisi work design.

Examples above show two pieces of Assisi work—one in traditional style, the other a modern version. The technique could be effectively adapted for a close-mesh canvas. Many cross stitch patterns can be adapted by reversing the position of stitch and background; it should always be remembered that Assisi work is essentially design in mass, not line.

TURKEY WORK

This is a form of hand-knotted wool embroidery on canvas, imitating the pile of Turkish carpet weaving. It was probably first used in England in the early 16th century and remained spasmodically in use until the late 17th century for loose cushions, chair seats and table carpets. It reappears occasionally for upholstery in the 18th century, and was known too in the 19th century.

It was certainly known in Colonial America, taken there most probably by English settlers. Patterns are always floral, stiffened and conventionalised.

NORWEAVE

Based on blocks of satin stitch worked on a canvas ground, this style of embroidery originated in Norway where it is known as Akle embroidery and is extremely popular in the Norwegian homes of today. The original design was inspired by traditional bedcovers woven in brightly coloured geometric patterns. All the designs are built up from blocks of stitches, which can vary in number and length depending upon whether a double thread or single thread canvas is used.

It is interesting that over the years the simple primary colours used originally have given way to vivid modern colours and that the designs have progressed from geometric, mosaic style patterns to a graphic style of design using flowers, birds and outdoor scenes as a new source of inspiration.

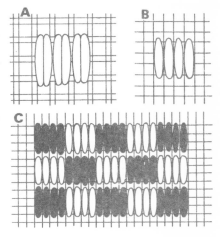

This type of embroidery has a wide variety of uses and in the chapter beginning on page 102 you will find a number of Norweave designs to make up.

If a double thread canvas is being used, then each block of stitches will consist of three double satin stitches over three double threads of the canvas (see diagram A). If a single thread canvas is being used, the blocks will each consist of four satin stitches worked over four threads of the canvas. (See diagram B). The blocks of stitches are worked side by side to form horizontal lines of stitchery across the entire canvas (diagram C).

church kneelers

Since time immemorial colour and pattern have been used in some form for the decoration of cathedrals and churches. Originally church art was a method of narrating the scriptures to the people but it is used today solely as a decoration and to give enhancement to a magnificent setting.

The church kneeler although functional in itself, has become a means of adding further ornamentation, colour and interest to the church's interior, and thus it has taken over a valuable dual role.

Canvas embroidery is the ideal technique for the making of kneelers, as it produces a firm, hardwearing fabric. Designs in all forms are acceptable—subtle traditional styles to blend with the mellow magnificence of age; or dramatic designs, vibrant with colour, to fit into a modern church interior.

Very often the making of kneelers for one church is under-taken by members of the congregation—men as well as women—as a combined and highly enjoyable communal project. Normally

one person will be appointed the overall designer in order to achieve a consistency of colour and pattern, and to ensure that the designs worked are harmonious as a whole, and in keeping with the church itself. Usually too the more experienced embroiderers take time and trouble to assist and advise the less experienced but no less enthusiastic workers. In this way, everyone contributes towards a common purpose, and a great deal of satisfaction and enjoyment are shared.

In the chapter beginning on page 102 you will find a number of kneeler designs to make up, including a double size kneeler for use by bride and groom at a wedding ceremony. It is however a fairly simple matter to adapt this to a single size kneeler if wished. Similarly the symbols on each kneeler are frequently interchangeable with those from another design.

If you are planning to make a number of kneelers for one church, it is often preferable for a theme to be followed either in colour scheme or design, or both. For this reason it is worth experimenting on paper at first, before committing needle to canvas, by interchanging symbols and pattern motifs from the different kneeler designs given.

Also, any of the designs given for kneelers can be fairly easily adapted to make alternative church furnishings such as choir seats, stool tops, cushions, pulpit falls, bible covers and collection bags.

PLANNING A DESIGN

There are several design points to bear in mind in relation to the working of kneelers. As with the working of cushions, the completed design should look good from any angle—and there should not be a 'right way up'. Also, and this is vitally important, when the kneeler is not in use, it will be hung up behind a pew—it is essential the design is as pleasing from this angle as when the kneeler is flat on the floor. It is not necessary to use complicated stitches to achieve a good result, provided the simple stitches chosen are carefully, neatly and evenly executed.

Before embarking on a finished design, work several small samples on different mesh sizes of canvas, with a variety of threads, until you are satisfied you have found the best combination for your design. Or, if you are supervising a team of workers, then from the assorted samplers made you can choose the right design for the right worker, bearing in mind his or her ability and experience in needlework. Crewel wool or any similar substantial thread should be used as it is usually moth-proof and is sturdy and hardwearing.

The average size of a completed kneeler is around 9in. by 12in. by 3in. deep. Generally, as with stools (see page 65), it is normal for the top area of the kneeler to contain a complete design motif, the sides are either plain or incorporate a motif related to the main top motif. You can either make your kneeler as one complete piece, or in five separate pieces—one piece for the top, four strips for the sides.

It is preferable—and easier—to make up the kneeler in one piece. The diagram on page 65 shows the shape of piece you will work. Embroidery is worked within the outer lines, so you have four corner areas of unworked canvas.

If you are making up one of the designs in the chapter which

An example of a kneeler made as a combined church project. The embroidery has been completed, and now the kneeler is ready to be made up.

begins on page 102, you will find in most cases that the pattern chart will give the top, one short side and one long side only—you must remember to add on the two remaining sides and work them to match the corresponding sections given.

Whether you work your kneeler in one piece, or in five separate sections, it is a reasonably easy matter to increase the depth of the side sections if wished. If there is only plain background on the pieces then there is no problem—simply work the required number of extra rows. If a motif is included in the side pieces however, work them as given and add extra depth to background equally on either side of the motif. As a guide when calculating the quantity of extra wool required, very approximately 7yd. of tapestry wool would be required to complete a 2in. square in trammed tent stitch on canvas with a mesh of 10 holes to the inch.

If you are devising your own kneeler design, calculate total yarn required by method given for stools on page 65.

MAKING-UP

Prepare and frame-up your canvas in the usual way, as described on pages 33 and 34, then work embroidery in chosen pattern taking care to work stitches evenly and giving a good coverage to canvas on both sides. Do not forget that the kneeler will have to withstand long and constant wear.

When the embroidery is completed, stretch the canvas thoroughly (see page 63). Leave it to dry completely—up to two or even three weeks, if necessary. It is vital this stage is not rushed. Time spent on stretching and the finishing touches will be amply repaid in terms of durability of your work.

When the canvas is dry and you are satisfied it has been sufficiently stretched, trim the unworked edges to $\frac{3}{4}$in. from the embroidery (including corner areas). Oversew these edges immediately to prevent fraying.

Stitch corners together, with right sides facing, using a strong

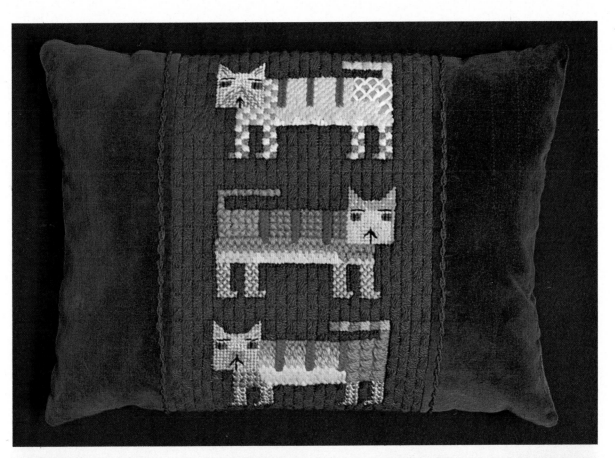

Top: three cat cushion (see page 162). Below: Norweave picture (see page 130).

Geometric-patterned cushion (see page 103).

linen upholstery thread in a colour to match the canvas itself, and stitching with a neat back stitch seam close to the embroidery. When the kneeler is turned right side out, no canvas should show through on the right side of work. If you have made your kneeler in five pieces, then stitch side sections to top section first, also with right side together and using a neat back stitch seam, then stitch corner seams, as for kneeler made in one piece.

The pad for your kneeler should be a very firm resilient substance such as a dense rubber sorbo. Cover it firmly with a wrapping of strong hessian or calico and stitch covering securely in place. Now turn your embroidered cover the right way out and fit it over your covered pad. Stuff a little cotton wool into each of the corners to make a good firm shape. There should be no loose unfilled areas of fabric at all—the finished kneeler should be very tightly stuffed in every part. It is best to have a pad which is about $\frac{1}{2}$in. larger all round than the measurement you are working to for the embroidery. This will ensure a good tight fit.

Fold turnings of unworked canvas to base of pad and using a strong upholstery linen thread, lace top and bottom edges together, and the two side edges together. If canvas shows on line of edges, a row of back stitch will cover it.

If the kneeler is to be hung when not in use, two 16in. lengths of 1in. wide carpet binding should be slipped through the ring and sewn on to backing in a fan shape (see diagram, right). Position the ring in centre of one short side edge.

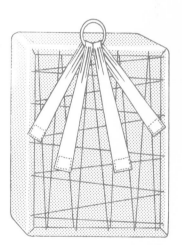

Finally cut a piece of lining fabric to fit base, plus $\frac{1}{2}$in. on all edges for seam allowance. Use a strong furnishing fabric, tailor's linen or furnishing velvet. Turn in seam allowance, place fabric to base of kneeler, wrong sides together and oversew neatly in position round all edges.

SYMBOLS USED ON KNEELERS

Christian symbols are an important element used in the design for kneelers. Such symbols were used by the early Christians as a picture language to convey secret messages. Many were taken from existing pagan symbols, others developed slowly alongside the growth of the church.

The cross in its many forms is probably the most well known symbol of all, and as it is also a geometric form it lends itself well to a canvas embroidery. The form of the cross grew from early origins and is formed by a vertical straight line which represents light, otherwise fire, striking from heaven, crossing the horizontal line which represents water. Fire and water thus become united, to symbolise creation.

The Calvary or passion cross incorporating the circle (see the cross in York Kneeler, page 144, and in the centre of the bridal kneeler, page 108) was not generally used as a symbol in Christianity until the fifth century and replaced the Chi Rho (see overleaf). The circle stands for no beginning and no end, and continues to symbolise the meaning of eternity.

Overleaf is a selection of well-known symbols which recur frequently on all forms of church decoration. Each symbol is presented in chart form so you may if you wish adapt it to fit into a kneeler design.

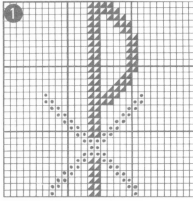

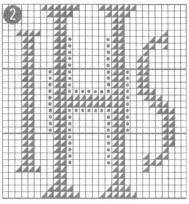

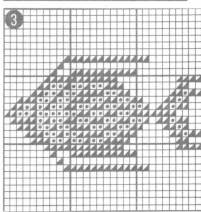

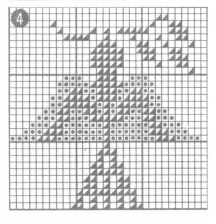

1. **The Chi Rho.** The earliest monogram of Christ both in eastern and western churches; it was often combined with other symbols.

2. **I.H.S.** This is generally taken to be the initial letters of Iesus Hominum Salvator—Jesus Saviour of Man. This gradually replaced the Chi Rho.

3. **The Fish.** One of the secret symbols used by early Chirstians. The initial letters of the Greek words for Jesus Christ, Son of God, Saviour, form together the Greek word for fish. Three fish together symbolise baptism.

4. **The Dove.** Sometimes tne dove is seen with a halo; since earliest time, the dove has represented the Holy Spirit. The dove with the olive branch symbolises peace.

5. **Tongues of Flames of Fire.** This represents the coming of the Holy Spirit.

6. **Three Circles.** The circles should be interlaced to represent the Trinity: God the Father, God the Son, and God the Holy Spirit. The three eternal beings in unity.

7. **The Double Triangle.** The seal of Solomon, representing the perfect God and perfect man.

8. **The Chalice, Alpha and Omega.** The Chalice is used to symbolise the Passion. Alpha and Omega are the first and last letters of the Greek alphabet, and so symbolise the beginning and the end.

9. **The Pentalpha.** The five-pointed star of Bethlehem. It stands for the descent into matter and for man as the Son of God. It was the attitude of prayer and still is in the eastern Church.

10. **The Ship.** Riding amidst storms, the ships represents the image of the church, particularly in the early days of Christianity.

11. **The Sun.** The source of light and heat, it has been accepted as a symbol of the Son of Righteousness.

12. **The Crescent·Moon.** This is the symbol of Byzantium, and represents the feminine principle. It is the symbol of the Virgin, who is often represented with a crescent moon, horns upwards, at her feet. The sun and moon together have the joint symbolism of the dual principle, day and night, male and female, birth and death throughout eternity.

13. **The Crown.** This denotes kingly power.

14. **The Corn.** Representing the source of the staff of life.

15. **The Anchor.** This was a very early symbol and when terminating in a cross meant steadfastness and hope. An anchor and fish signify that the Christian's hope lies in Christ.

16. **The Rose.** This is an emblem of love and beauty, and is consecrated to the Virgin.

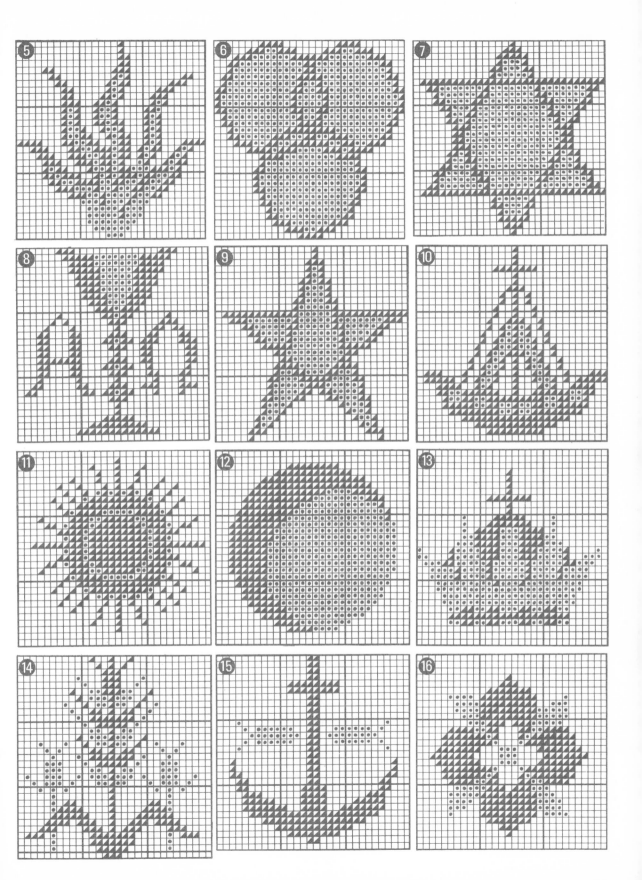

the importance of design

Once a knowledge of the basic elements of stitchery and the characteristics of canvas have been acquired, you will want to go on to create your own canvas work designs, and to experiment with threads, textures, and combinations of stitches.

ADAPTING A MOTIF

As a start, before creating a new design in entirety, try adapting an existing motif—choose a motif from one of the designs to make in the chapter beginning on page 102. For instance, if you like a particular design, but would prefer to make it into a different finished article, perhaps a handbag rather than a cushion, it is a simple matter to draft a new pattern on graph paper. Ideally, choose a grid of graph paper to match the mesh of your canvas—i.e. if you are using a canvas with a mesh of 10 holes to the inch, then use graph paper with 10 squares to the inch. This will give you a diagram in the actual size of the finished design.

On the graph paper draw out shape and size of the article you wish to make (the outline of the shape, not the design motif). This will then give the number of stitches both lengthwise and

Example of an exploded circle design, worked in a variety of stitches and threads.

Four tapestry embroidered finger plates, each worked in cross stitch on double thread canvas, 10 holes to the inch. Penelope Designs P/F520, P/F517, P/F518 and P/F519.

widthwise. Count the squares on the chart given for the design and calculate if it will fit happily into your outline—if you think it will, then mark it out on your graph paper within the outline you have drawn.

When the overall areas of the canvas required for the complete design and background have been calculated, cut the canvas with a 3in. margin all round, to allow for the final stretching and mounting. Follow the chart you have drafted for working the design.

It is possible to enlarge or reduce a given design by using a different mesh size of canvas—use one with more holes to the inch than the one quoted in the pattern and this will make the design smaller, fewer holes to the inch will make the design larger.

Where a design consists of a number of repeated motifs, the motif can be isolated then a number of motifs arranged in an alternative pattern from the one given. The diagrams below show some ideas for adapting a motif in this way.

In diagram A, a motif measuring 5in. by 3in. has been selected—the first sketch shows an arrangement of eight repeats of the motif; the second sketch shows a central strip of three motifs; and in the third sketch, two groups of two motifs are used. Each of these shapes could be used for a cushion or for a chair or stool top.

Diagram B shows a treatment for a floral motif. In the first sketch, two motifs are linked close together and are used along each edge of a cushion. The second sketch, for a firescreen, shows two vertical strips of motifs—in each strip the motif is repeated four times, with the direction of alternate motifs reversed, to give an apparently continuous line of flowers.

Diagram C shows three alternative arrangements for a geometric motif. And diagram D gives an even more ambitious adaptation—the first sketch shows a circular centre motif used for a wall hanging or firescreen. In the second sketch one 'leg' of the complete motif has been selected and used as a repeated border, worked in alternate directions, for a stool top.

DIAGRAM A **DIAGRAM B** **DIAGRAM C** **DIAGRAM D**

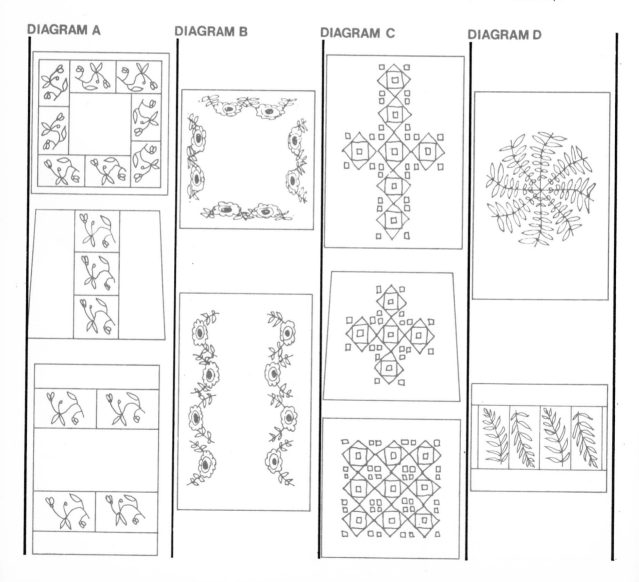

GEOMETRIC DESIGNS

By now you should have acquired a 'taste' for designing, and you can take the first steps to creating your own designs. Because canvas embroidery is bound by the limitations of a squared canvas, geometric shapes are ideally suited to the work.

Begin therefore by doodling on a sheet of graph paper—the squares of the graph paper will impose the same limitations as the canvas. Try simply filling in squares, diamonds, rectangles, and other elementary geometric shapes until you find one which is pleasing. Then try working it on a small piece of canvas, perhaps using only one colour of thread, and one stitch—cross stitch, for instance—just as a simple experiment to give you the feeling for transposing design from paper to canvas.

Next try the same design in a different combination of thread colours—perhaps using different colours within the motif itself. And try working in different stitches. This all helps to familiarise you with stitching technique and design, and the limitations of the canvas itself. Remember always to 'block in' areas of design with colours or stitches: outlined designs are not suitable for canvas technique.

Now move on to the next more ambitious stage of designing— combining different geometric shapes in the one design. If the thought of being confronted with a sheet of blank paper and pencil is frightening, try instead cutting squares and triangles and other similar geometrical shapes from coloured paper.

Place these shapes on a sheet of white paper and move them around in different arrangements until you find a pattern which pleases you. This will produce a more spontaneous result than any laboured drawing of lines. When arranging the shapes, remember too that the spaces left should be as balanced and pleasing as the shapes themselves. The diagram on the right shows one possible arrangement of geometric shapes. After you have cut out your squares, triangles or whatever, do not throw away the scraps of paper left over—try to make another pattern arrangement with them. Diagram below, right, shows an arrangement of the 'leftover' shapes from the design, left.

Sampler worked in a pleasing arrangement of geometric shapes, mainly in rice, cross and tent stitches.

A boring design would result if you have all the spaces—or for that matter the shapes themselves—of similar width and size. Vary the proportions experimentally until you find an arrangement which is pleasing.

When you are satisfied you have arrived at a suitable arrangement, place a sheet of tracing paper over the arrangement and trace off the outline of your design.

Transfer the design to your canvas either by the painting

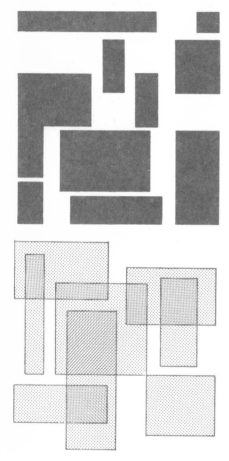

method (see page 69) or the graph paper method as described on pages 70 and 73.

Now try another experiment in geometric design: cut out a square from coloured paper, and from this square cut out smaller squares and rectangles and spread these cut-out shapes out on a sheet of plain paper without actually re-arranging their positions. This is the design principle known as an 'exploded' square. The pincushion illustrated on page 141 is a good example of this design principle.

Vary the spaces between each cut-out shape so you become aware of the shape of the space left in relation to the shape of the piece of paper. The diagram, left, shows an example of an exploded square design.

Transfer the design to your canvas by either the painting or graph paper method (see pages 69 and 70).

Now try overlapping geometric shapes, thereby producing shapes within the original shapes. Cut out from tissue paper similar geometric shapes as for previous experiments, and arrange them to form a pleasing design but this time overlap some of the pieces.

When you are satisfied with the arrangement, use transparent self-adhesive tape to stick them in position to the sheet of backing paper, then place tracing paper over the whole arrangement, and trace off the design, tracing the overlapping outlines as well as the outer edges. Transfer to your canvas by either the painting or graph paper method (see pages 69 and 70).

Different stitches and colours of thread can be used to emphasise the shapes within shapes.

It is very important when devising a design to remember that the shape of the design motif should be related to the shape to be filled. For example, a square should not be fitted into a rectangular shape—the design chosen to fill a rectangular outline should also be rectangular in form.

Any design based on geometric forms, such as outlined so far, can be easily adapted to form the pattern for a pincushion, stool top or cushion. At the same time this gives good grounding and practice in the use of stitches. With constant practice, you will soon learn how to adapt these stitches to fit into a more intricate design, which may in fact involve using only half a particular stitch at the edge of a shape or using tent stitch to fill in edges of a design.

While still working in the experimental stages it is best to avoid designs using circles, curves and un-true diagonals as these conflict with the limitations of the canvas technique.

INSPIRATIONS FROM NATURAL SOURCES

Once you have acquired a working knowledge of design principles in relation to geometric shapes and outlines, begin to look around you for inspiration. You will be surprised how many everyday objects can offer inspiration—the particular pattern of a brick or stone wall, for instance, a decorative facade on a building, a stained glass window—even an arrangement of several branches of a tree outlined against the sky. All can be adapted and translated into a canvas work design.

Plants, birds, insects, animals, even a landscape can be the inspiration for a canvas design. In every case however the original shape must be broken down into suitable geometric forms—the three cat cushion on page 89 demonstrates the adapting of the elegant shape of a cat into a canvas work motif.

Buildings—both ancient and modern—are another source of inspiration for design, and are particularly suitable as their shapes are also usually based on squares and rectangles.

Never copy—or try to copy—nature implicitly, but adapt a natural form and use it to produce an individual interpretation suitable for the medium in which you are working.

Seedheads and fruit provide another storehouse of inspiration. As a start, cut them through the middle and use the inside as a basis for a design—a cut apple, or a green pepper, for instance, can produce an exciting and original design. See illustration on page 36.

Select just one particular part of a flower—maybe the centre—and use this as a starting off point for a design. Or one section of a leaf to fill the whole area and forget the complete outline of the leaf. Use the beautiful design on the wing of an insect, a butterfly, for instance, and forget about the insect in its complete form.

INSPIRATION FROM OTHER MEDIUMS

Other art forms can also provide sources of inspiration, both historical examples and modern ones. Perhaps you may not have the patience—or the time—to interpret exactly an intricate and detailed piece of Elizabethan carving, for instance, but the essential characteristics of the design, its outline and basic form can most probably be simplified and adapted to give a pleasing and attractive piece of work.

Similarly, a design worked in knitting or in crochet (which is also, as is canvas work, based on squares) or in macramé (especially Cavandoli work which was originally inspired by cross stitch embroidery) can be most successfully adapted to the canvas embroidery technique.

A visit to a museum and careful study of the exhibits on view can be a rewarding experience. Take a notebook with you and jot down ideas as you see them. At home afterwards a few hours' thought and experimenting can produce some wonderfully vivid and inspired ideas for design.

COLOUR

Colour is of course all-important in planning any design—and as much for canvas work as for any other artistic form.

It is better to work out an all over colour scheme before commencing the piece of work rather than select colours for individual areas of the design. A more pleasing and consistent effect will be achieved if time is spent experimenting with colours beforehand.

Restrict the colours in a particular design to two only, with a variation of shades of those colours. Try to avoid having an equal amount of each colour as this produces a somewhat tedious design. A tiny touch of a third colour can add interest and highlight the piece.

For example, try a design with the majority of shades in pink, a slightly lesser number of shades of orange and just a touch of white.

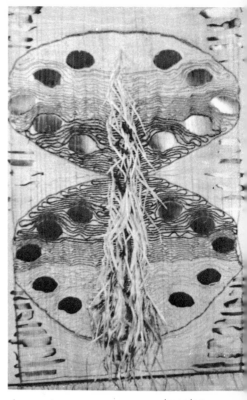

A contemporary woven hanging, worked with unusual materials, including string, hemp, charred veneers and X-ray plates.

Before you embark on a design, rough out an approximate plan of where the colours are to be placed, although there are bound to be changes as the work evolves.

Try never to be restricted by the natural colour of the subject of your design but try above all to produce an interesting and well-balanced design. For example, if the whole piece is embroidered in shades of orange and brown a green summer leaf can be turned into an autumn one.

ADAPTING A DESIGN

Once you find a particular design idea which pleases you, it can be adapted in limitless ways and in different shapes and sizes and forms. The ideas for using different arrangements of repeated motifs on page 96 clearly show one possible adaptation. Similarly the instructions for enlarging, widening or reducing a design on pages 73 and 74 will also help to give more 'mileage' to a design idea.

If you are working a design for a border edging, a simple way to form a regular and symmetrical corner area is to place a mirror diagonally across the design and follow the reflection thus given for the corner part of the design. Alternatively if you want to devise a perfect squared motif, then place two mirrors at right angles to each other across the motif, and you should then get a reflection of a squared-up area of the design. A mirror is in fact very helpful in experimenting with design repeats—to see which are effective, and which are not.

WORKING WITH OTHER MATERIALS

Pleasing work can be done by combining canvas embroidery judiciously with other materials and with other craft forms—collage, for instance, felt work or appliqué. Try as a start incorporating wooden beads or even sea-shells with holes drilled in them into a design—just stitch the bead or shell on to your canvas at the point where you want it to appear. Try also couching threads on to the canvas if they are too thick to be stitched in place, or if they are interesting textured threads.

Soon you find practically any oddment—natural or man-made—will be useful for a canvas work design. You will become an insatiable hoarder of pieces of tree bark and cork, fabric oddments, even pebbles from the beach . . . all will be carefully cleaned and put aside for future use.

Materials such as leather, suede, gold or imitation gold kid can be incorporated into a canvas design. Attractive shapes should be cut out from the material and then stitched in place to the canvas, if necessary padding the shapes first with felt or wool so they do not sink into the canvas.

Although it is interesting to experiment by combining apparently dissimilar techniques and objects, never use an object or idea merely as a gimmick. This destroys all the important elements of design. In other words, every technique, fabric, item or idea you use must contribute something towards the finished design. A group of buttons stitched to a piece of embroidery should never, for instance, look like a group of buttons, and bear no relation to the work as a whole.

Experiment further afield and try working on backgrounds other than the conventional canvas—gingham, for instance, can give a most interesting backing for a piece of cross stitch work. Treat the squares in the gingham pattern as you would the squares of the canvas, and work stitches accordingly. This can provide a most attractive edging for a dress.

Net, too, which is composed of interlaced fibres can give a basis for fine canvas stitching, and it is also extremely effective. Pleasing work can also be done on hessian (see right). Any metal grid, including chicken wire, can have bold stitches worked over it to give an unusual and dramatic modern embroidery. Much experimental work of this nature has been done in recent years by art students, some of the work very impressive indeed.

Alternatively any fabric can have canvas stitches worked on it, if canvas is first tacked over the material to be decorated. Then the canvas stitches, as required, are worked through the double thickness of canvas and fabric. When the design is complete, the threads of the canvas are cut and very carefully removed one by one. The design, beautifully even and uniform, then remains in place on the linen or whatever fabric has been chosen.

Care must be taken not actually to pierce the canvas with the needle when the embroidery is being done, for if such a mistake occurs it would be very difficult to remove the threads of the canvas afterwards. The only danger with this technique is that sometimes stitches are rather loose against the fabric.

Although the golden rule of canvas embroidery is to ensure that every part of the canvas ground is covered by stitching, effective designs can be evolved by leaving areas of the canvas actually unworked so they become an intrinsic part of the complete design. Alternatively, back a section of the canvas with a suitable textured fabric—hessian, perhaps—before beginning work, then pull or cut away this area of the canvas itself to reveal the hessian backing.

Once experience has been gained in canvas work, and a thorough knowledge of stitching techniques acquired, it is worth experimenting with design. Keep to the rules—to start with at any rate—and aim for a result which is attractive, harmonious and in keeping with the medium being used. Only constant experimenting, and trial and error can show what is right—and what is wrong.

Canvas work design worked on a hessian ground.

designs to make

In every pattern in this chapter specific thread and fabric colours are quoted. These are intended merely as a guide to the design we made up. The colours may, of course, be altered to suit personal preference, and the purpose for which the finished item is required.

The USA equivalents for yarns quoted in the patterns are given on page 176.

Fall, tapestry embroidered picture; Penelope Design F/P459.

geometric-patterned cushion

Illustrated in colour on page 90.

MATERIALS

Of Coats Anchor Tapisserie Wool—16 skeins White 0402, 3 skeins Cyclamen 089, 3 skeins Deep Maroon 0873, 2 skeins Mid Grey 0398, and 2 skeins Brown 0904. $\frac{1}{2}$yd. double thread tapestry canvas. 19in. wide, 10 holes to 1in. $\frac{1}{2}$yd. white medium-weight furnishing fabric, 48in. wide, for backing. Milward 'Gold Seal' tapestry needle No. 19. A cushion pad 15in. by 12$\frac{1}{2}$in.

MEASUREMENTS

Finished cushion measures approximately 15$\frac{1}{2}$in. by 13in.

DIAGRAMS (see pages 104 and 105).

Diagram A gives one quarter of the complete design. Each background square on the diagram represents the double thread of the canvas. (**Note.** Turn diagram so short edges are at the sides, the patterned section is along the top.)

Diagram B shows the arrangement of the stitches on the threads of the canvas. The double stitches are the cross stitches; the small, separate stitches are the half cross stitches which are worked over single threads of the canvas.

STITCHES

Cross
Half cross

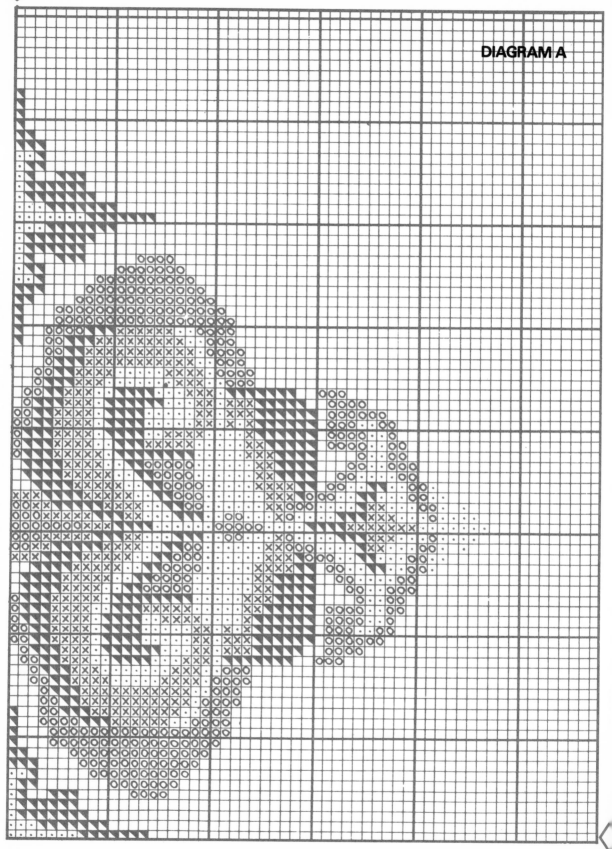

DIAGRAM A

TO MAKE

Mark the centre of canvas both ways with a line of basting stitches. Take stitches along a line of holes lengthwise and between a pair of narrow double threads widthwise. Prepare canvas, and mount it, if you are using a frame.

The design is worked in cross stitch and half cross stitch. With one long side of canvas facing you, commence embroidery centrally and work the quarter of the design given in diagram A, following stitch and colour key and diagram A. The blank arrows on the diagram mark the centre and should coincide with your basting stitches. To complete work other three quarters to correspond.

TO COMPLETE

Stretch canvas if necessary.

Trim canvas to within 1in. of embroidery. Cut a piece the same size from backing fabric. Place fabric and embroidery together, right sides facing, and sew round 3 sides close to the embroidery (no canvas should show when cover is turned right side out). Turn cover to right side. Insert cushion pad. Turn in remaining seam allowance along open edges and slipstitch neatly together.

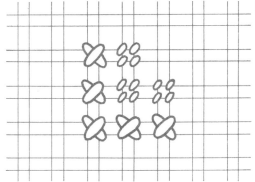

DIAGRAM B

STITCH AND COLOUR KEY

Mid Grey cross stitch
White cross stitch
Brown cross stitch
Cyclamen Half cross stitch
Deep Maroon Half cross stitch

Note. 1 cross stitch = 1 square on the diagram
4 half cross stitches = 1 square on the diagram

fireside stool

Illustrated opposite.

MATERIALS

Of Coats Anchor Tapisserie Wool—13 skeins Magenta 064, 8 skeins Tangerine 0313, 7 skeins Flame 0333, and 6 skeins Petunia 0417. $\frac{5}{8}$yd. single thread tapestry canvas, 23in. wide, 18 threads to 1in. 1$\frac{5}{8}$yd. furnishing velvet or similar mediumweight fabric, 48in. wide, to match magenta thread colour. 2$\frac{1}{4}$yd. thick cord, $\frac{1}{2}$in. thick, also to match magenta shade (alternatively a cord can be made from 12 skeins of tapisserie wool). 4 tassels to match cord, each approximately $\frac{7}{8}$in. long (similarly, tassels can be made from 13 skeins of tapisserie wool). Stool pad to fit (see measurements below). Milward 'Gold Seal' tapestry needle No. 19.

MEASUREMENTS

Finished fireside stool measures approximately 18in. square and 16in. deep.

STITCHES

Tent
Brick
Satin

Right: bridal kneeler (see page 132).
Below: fender stool (see page 128).

DIAGRAM (see pages 110 and 111).
Diagram A gives one quarter of the complete design. The background lines on the diagram represent the threads of the canvas. (**Note.** This diagram has been separated into two equal sections. Both sections should have centre edges placed together to give complete diagram A.)

TO MAKE
Mark the centre of canvas both ways with a line of basting stitches. Prepare canvas, and mount it, if you are using a frame (it is strongly recommended for this design that a frame is used).

Begin embroidery centrally and work the quarter given in diagram A, following stitch and colour key and diagram A. The blank arrows on the diagram mark the centre and should coincide with your basting stitches. It will be necessary to work with the side of the frame facing to complete the area of brick stitch at right-hand side of diagram A. However if a table or floor frame is used the same area of brick stitch will have to be in rows of horizontal stitches, worked alternately from top to bottom. Work other three quarters to correspond.

TO COMPLETE
Stretch canvas if necessary.
Trim canvas to within 1in. of embroidery. Cut from the fabric 2 pieces, each 40in. by 18in., for the sides, and one piece 20in. square for the base. Place the side pieces round the fireside stool pad with the right side of fabric inwards. Keep the raw edges to the outside and pin short ends together to fit pad snugly. Carefully remove from pad and stitch these seams. Trim turnings, and press seams open. Baste embroidered canvas to top of fabric side section, right sides together, and seams coinciding with corners. Stitch close to embroidery. Turn to right side and place over the pad. Trim base section of fabric to fit pad, allowing $\frac{1}{2}$in. on all edges for turnings. Turn in this seam allowance round all edges and slip stitch in position. Stitch cord in position round edge of top embroidered section. Attach a tassel to each corner.

STITCH AND COLOUR KEY
Magenta Tent stitch

Petunia Tent stitch

Tangerine Brick stitch

Flame Brick stitch

Tangerine Satin stitch

Flame Satin stitch

Petunia Satin stitch

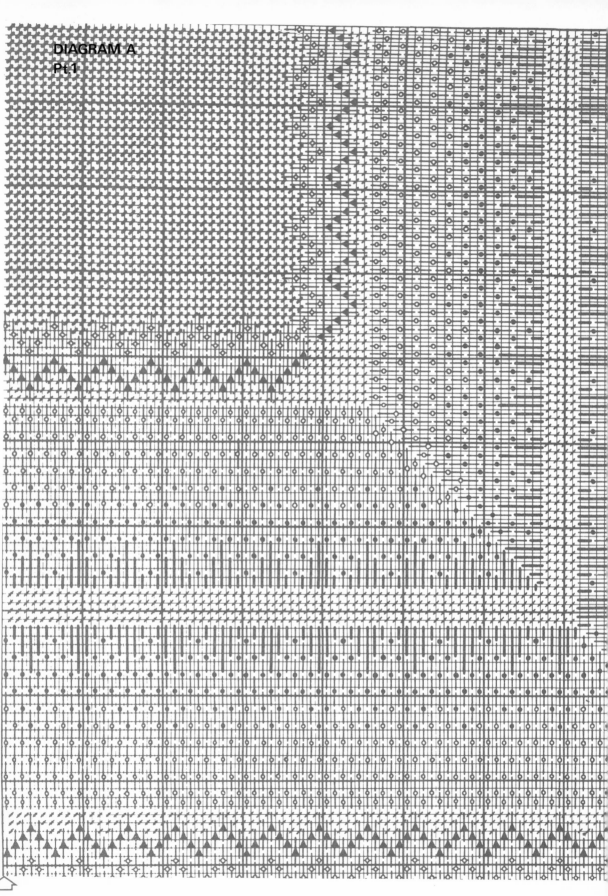

DIAGRAM A
Pt.1

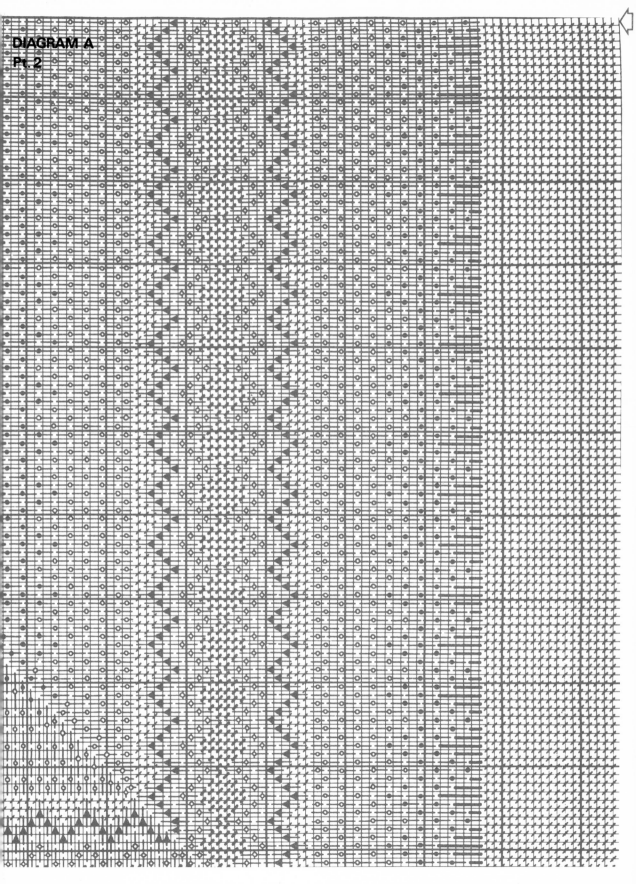

DIAGRAM A
Pt. 2

head cushion

Illustrated in colour on page 126.

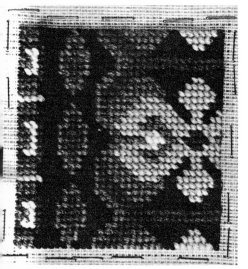

STITCH
Trammed tent

COLOUR KEY
- [X] Magenta
- [•] Kingfisher
- [/] Jade
- [ ] White
- [◣] Black

MATERIALS
Of Coats Anchor Tapisserie Wool—13 skeins Jade 0187, 4 skeins Kingfisher 0158, 4 skeins Black 0403, 3 skeins Magenta 064, and 1 skein White 0402. $\frac{1}{2}$yd. double thread tapestry canvas, 23in. wide, 10 holes to 1in. $\frac{3}{8}$yd. mediumweight close-weave furnishing fabric, 48in. wide, to match Jade tapisserie wool. 12 oz. lead shot for counterweight straps. A cushion pad approximately 17$\frac{1}{2}$in. by 11in. Milward 'Gold Seal' tapestry needle No. 19.

MEASUREMENTS
Finished cushion (excluding straps) measures 18in. by 11$\frac{1}{2}$in.

DIAGRAM
Diagram A gives a little more than a quarter of the complete design. Each background square on the diagram represents the double threads of the canvas. (**Note.** Turn diagram so short edges are at the sides, the patterned section is along the top.)

TO MAKE
Mark the centre of canvas both ways with a line of basting stitches. Take stitches along a line of holes lengthwise and between a pair of narrow double threads widthwise. Prepare canvas, and mount it, if you are using a frame. With one long side of canvas facing you, commence embroidery centrally and work the quarter of the design given in diagram A, following colour key and diagram A. The blank arrows on the diagram mark the centre and should coincide with your basting stitches. The design is worked throughout in trammed tent stitch. To complete design, work other three quarters to correspond.

TO COMPLETE
Stretch canvas if necessary.
Trim canvas to within 1in. of embroidery. Cut from the backing fabric 2 pieces, each 26in. by 5$\frac{1}{2}$in. for straps, and one piece the same size as trimmed canvas. Fold each strap section in half lengthwise, right sides together, and taking $\frac{1}{2}$in. turnings, machine stitch long side and one short end. Trim and clip turnings, and turn right side out. Insert equal quantities of lead shot into each strap.
With right side uppermost and one long side of embroidery facing you, pin straps in position with raw edges level at the top, and each strap 3$\frac{1}{2}$in. from raw side edges. Place right side of backing section to right side of embroidery, thus sandwiching straps between, and sew close to the embroidery leaving lower edge unstitched. Turn to right side, insert pad, turn in seam allowance along lower edge and slipstitch neatly together.

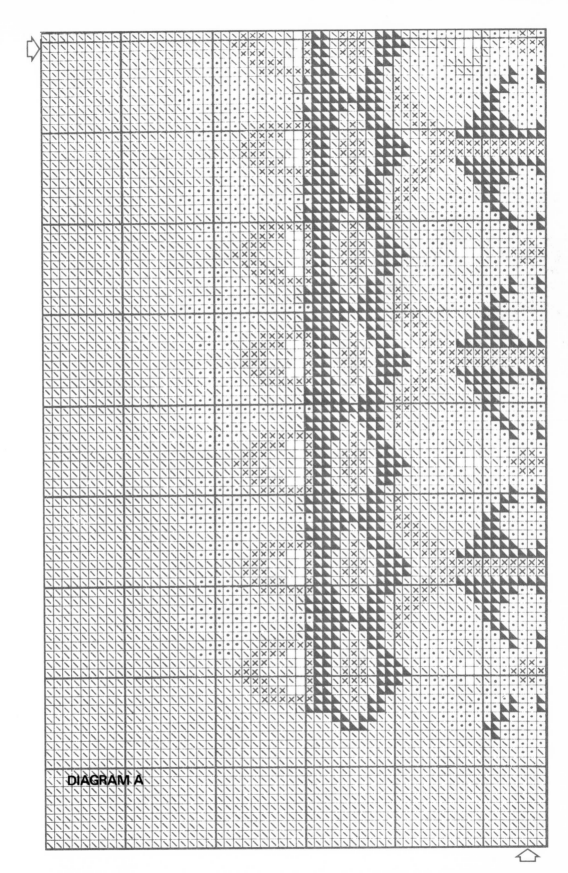

DIAGRAM A

bell pull

Illustrated in colour on page 126.

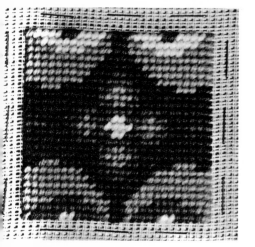

MATERIALS
Of Coats Anchor Tapisserie Wool—10 skeins Cyclamen 089, 7 skeins Flame (medium) 0332, 7 skeins Flame (dark) 0335, 3 skeins White 0402. 1¼yd. double thread tapestry canvas, 19in. wide, 10 holes to 1in. ¼yd. orange mediumweight furnishing fabric, 48in. wide, for backing. Bell pull attachment to fit each end of embroidered panel. Milward 'Gold Seal' tapestry needle No. 19.

MEASUREMENTS
Finished size of bell pull is approximately 40in. by 5¼in.

DIAGRAM
Diagram A gives a section of the complete design. Each background square on the diagram represents the double threads of the canvas.

TO MAKE
Mark the centre of canvas both ways with a line of basting stitches. Take stitches along a line of holes lengthwise and between a pair of narrow double threads widthwise. Prepare canvas, and mount it, if you are using a frame. Commence embroidery centrally and work the lower half of the complete design. Work bracketed section A as given on diagram A first, following colour key and diagram A. The blank arrows on the diagram mark the centre and should coincide with your basting stitches. Repeat section A once more immediately below, then work section B to finish lower half of the bell pull. To complete the upper half of the design, work section A twice, then complete top edge to correspond with section B.

TO COMPLETE
Stretch canvas if necessary.
Trim canvas to within 1in. of embroidery. Cut a piece from fabric the same size as trimmed canvas. Place both pieces together. right sides facing, and sew down each long side close to the embroidery and to within 2in. of narrow ends. Turn to right side. Affix bell pull attachments to top and bottom by slipping canvas over the rods.
 Turn in canvas and stitch securely in position. Finish by turning in the remaining raw edges of backing neatly and slip-stitch to canvas.

STITCH
Trammed tent

A

B

COLOUR KEY
- ⊡ Cyclamen
- ☒ Medium Flame
- ◣ Dark Flame
- ☐ White

DIAGRAM A

florentine cushion

Illustrated in colour on page 143.

MATERIALS

Of Coats Anchor Tapisserie Wool—10 skeins Petunia (dark) 0417, 3 skeins Cyclamen (dark) 089, 2 skeins Cyclamen (light) 085, 2 skeins Brown (medium) 0379, 2 skeins Brown (dark) 0381, 1 skein Petunia (light) 095, 1 skein Beige (light) 0376, and 1 skein Beige (medium) 0377. $\frac{1}{2}$yd. single thread tapestry canvas, 23in. wide, 18 threads to 1in. $\frac{1}{2}$yd. velvet or similar mediumweight fabric, 36in. wide, to match Petunia (dark) Tapisserie Wool. A cushion pad approximately 14in. square. 2yd. cord, $\frac{1}{4}$in. thick, to match fabric. Milward 'Gold Seal' tapestry needle No. 19.

MEASUREMENTS

Finished cushion measures approximately 14in. square.

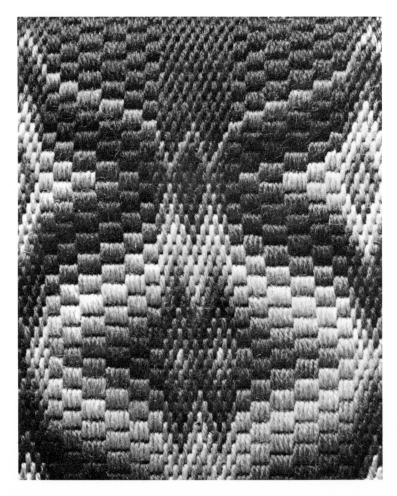

STITCH
Florentine (each stitch taken across number of horizontal threads of canvas as indicated on diagram A).

DIAGRAM (see pages 118 and 119).
Diagram A gives just under one quarter of design. The background lines on the diagram represent the threads of the canvas. To facilitate counting, every tenth background line has been made a little heavier. (**Note.** This design has been separated into two sections. Both sections should have centre edges placed together to give complete diagram A.)

TO MAKE
Mark the centre of canvas both ways with a line of basting stitches. Also, to facilitate counting, mark off threads in groups of ten (see page 33). Prepare canvas, and mount it, if you are using a frame.

Commence embroidery centrally at crossed basting stitches and work the section of the design given on diagram A, following colour key and diagram A—be sure to take each stitch across the correct number of threads as indicated on diagram. The blank arrows on the diagram mark the centre and should coincide with your basting stitches. Complete first quarter of the design by working background (dark petunia) to fill remaining area of canvas below section as given in diagram (i.e. 19 more threads of the canvas).

Work other three quarters of the design to correspond.

TO COMPLETE
Stretch canvas if necessary.

Trim canvas to within 1in. of embroidery. Cut a piece of backing fabric the same size as trimmed canvas. Place canvas and fabric pieces together, right sides facing, and sew close to the embroidery, round three sides. Turn right side out. Insert pad and turn in seam allowance along remaining edges. Slipstitch neatly together. Sew cord in position round the side seams, making a loop at each corner.

COLOUR KEY

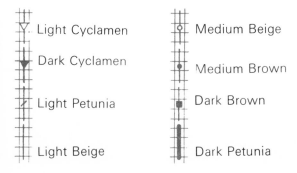

Light Cyclamen

Dark Cyclamen

Light Petunia

Light Beige

Medium Beige

Medium Brown

Dark Brown

Dark Petunia

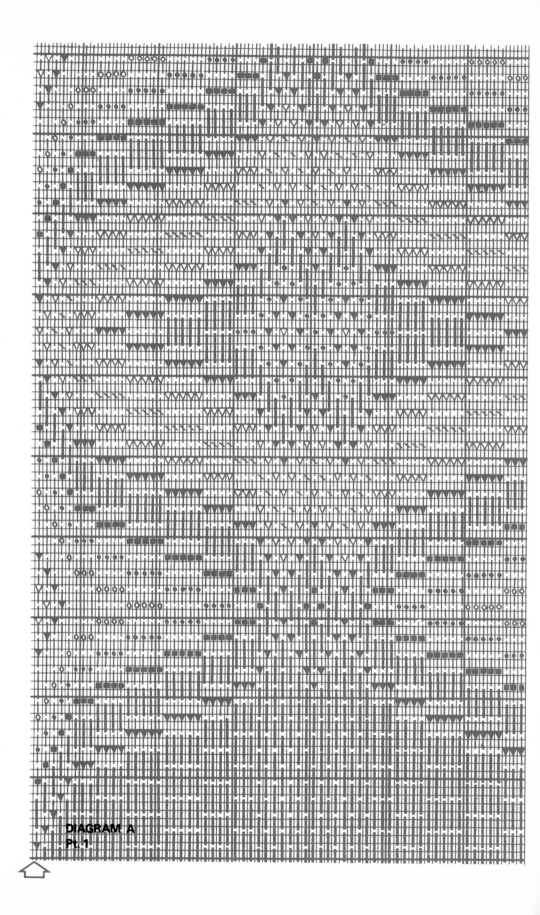

DIAGRAM A
Pt. 1

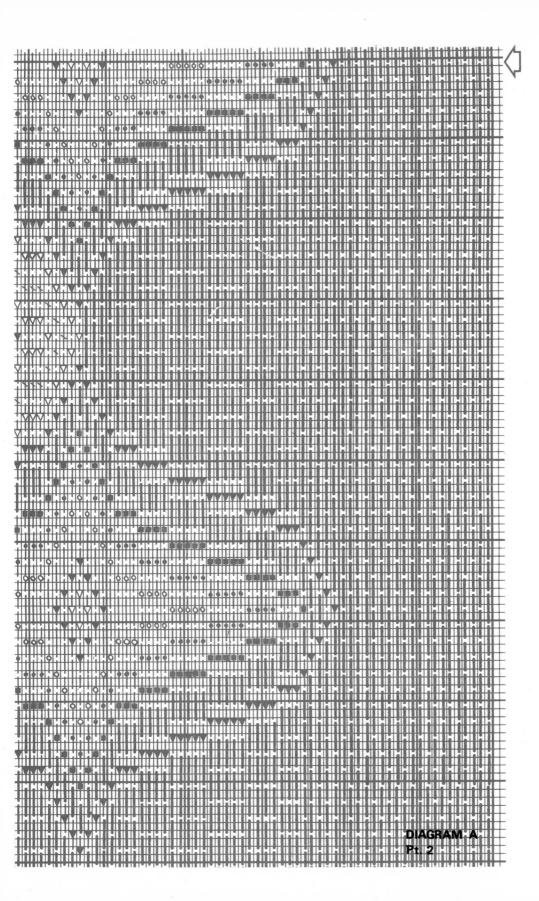

DIAGRAM A
Pt. 2

florentine stool top

Illustrated in colour on page 125.

MATERIALS

Of Coats Anchor Tapisserie Wool—6 skeins Peacock Blue 0167, 6 skeins Deep Blue 0850, 5 skeins Jade (light) 0185, 5 skeins Jade (medium) 0187, 5 skeins Smoke Blue 0849, 4 skeins Jade (dark) 0189, and 3 skeins Cobalt Blue 0159. $\frac{7}{8}$yd. single thread tapestry canvas, 23in. wide, 18 threads to 1in. Stool with an inset pad measuring 14in. by 24in. Milward 'Gold Seal' tapestry needle No. 19. Upholstery tacks.

MEASUREMENTS

Finished stool top measures 14in. by 24in.

STITCH
Florentine (each stitch is taken across 4 threads of the canvas as indicated on diagram A).

DIAGRAMS
Diagram 1 (overleaf) gives a section of the design, showing motifs A and B. The background lines on the diagram represent the threads of the canvas. (**Note.** This diagram has been separated into two sections. To make complete diagram, line up centre edges so top stitch of right-hand section forms 5th step up in Florentine sequence from 4 stitches on left-hand section.)
Diagram 2 (below) gives one quarter of the complete design, showing the position of the motifs.

TO MAKE
Mark the centre of canvas both ways with a line of basting stitches. Prepare the canvas, and mount it, if you are using a frame, but have the selvedges to the tapes instead of the cut edges, as the length of this design exceeds the width of the canvas. Turn in the surplus canvas at each side.

Commence the embroidery centrally, following diagram 1 and colour key. The blank arrows on the diagram mark the centre and should coincide with your basting stitches. Work the section given on diagram 1 first, then work a complete quarter of the complete design, following diagram 2 for position of motifs. The broken lines on diagram 2 indicate the centres, and these broken lines should coincide with your basting stitches. Work other three quarters to correspond.

TO COMPLETE
Stretch canvas if necessary.
Place the embroidery centrally on the stool pad, right side uppermost. Fold the unworked border of canvas back and secure in position on the underside with upholstery tacks.

COLOUR KEY

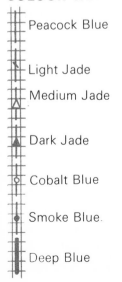

Peacock Blue

Light Jade

Medium Jade

Dark Jade

Cobalt Blue

Smoke Blue.

Deep Blue

DIAGRAM 2

121

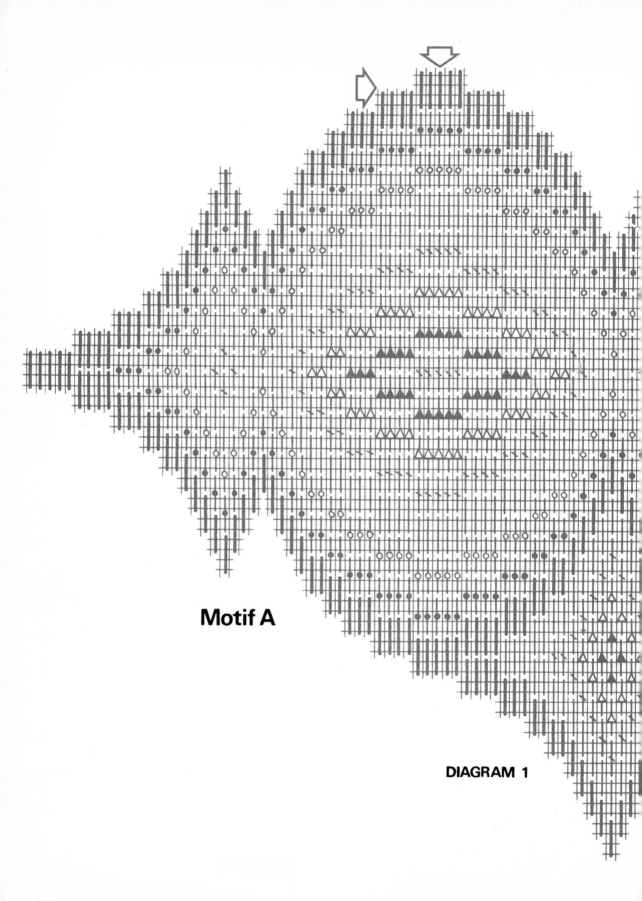

Motif A

DIAGRAM 1

122

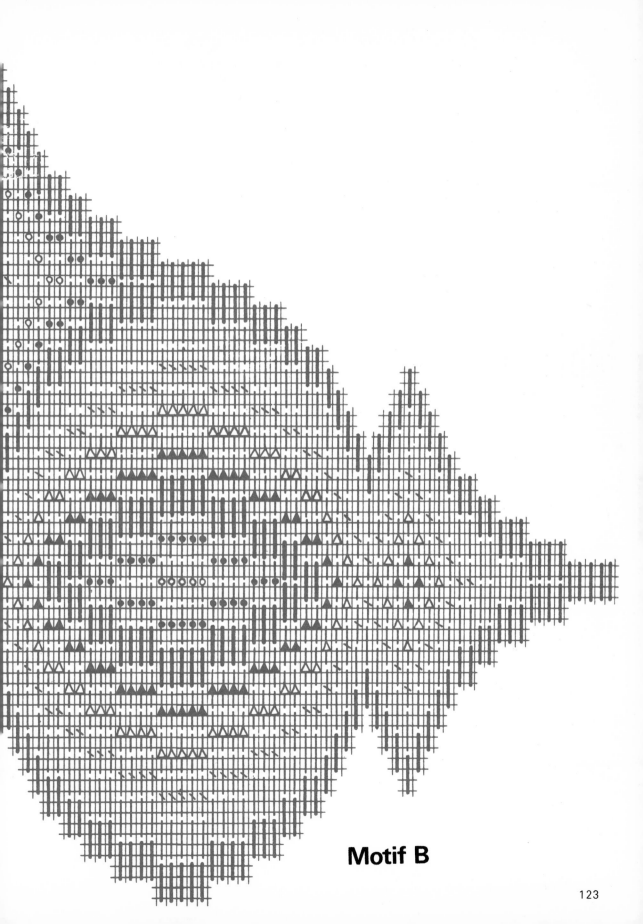

Motif B

norweave stool top

Illustrated opposite, below.

MATERIALS
Of Coats Anchor Tapisserie Wool—18 skeins Brown 0845, 7 skeins Amber Gold (pale) 0305, 4 skeins Amber Gold (dark) 0309, 3 skeins Flame 0332, and 1 skein Magenta 063. $\frac{5}{8}$yd. double thread tapestry canvas, 36in. wide, 10 holes to 1in. Stool with inset pad measuring $15\frac{1}{4}$in. by $23\frac{1}{4}$in. Milward 'Gold Seal' tapestry needle No. 19. Upholstery tacks.

MEASUREMENTS
Finished stool top measures $15\frac{1}{4}$in. by $23\frac{1}{4}$in.

STITCH
Satin stitch (worked in blocks of 3 double stitches, each pair of stitches worked over 3 double threads of the canvas).

DIAGRAM (see page 127)
Diagram A gives the complete design. Each background square on the diagram represents one block of 3 double satin stitches worked over 3 double threads of canvas.

TO MAKE
Trim the canvas to 20in. by 30in. Mark the centre both ways with a line of basting stitches. Take stitches along a line of holes widthwise, and between a pair of narrow double threads lengthwise. Prepare the canvas, and mount it, if you are using a frame.

Commence the embroidery centrally and work the design, following colour key and diagram A. The blank arrows on the diagram mark the centre and should coincide with your basting stitches.

TO COMPLETE
Stretch canvas if necessary.

Place the embroidery centrally on the stool pad, right side uppermost. Fold the unworked border of canvas back and secure on the underside of stool top with upholstery tacks.

COLOUR KEY
O	Magenta
	Pale Amber Gold
X	Dark Amber Gold
·	Flame
■	Brown

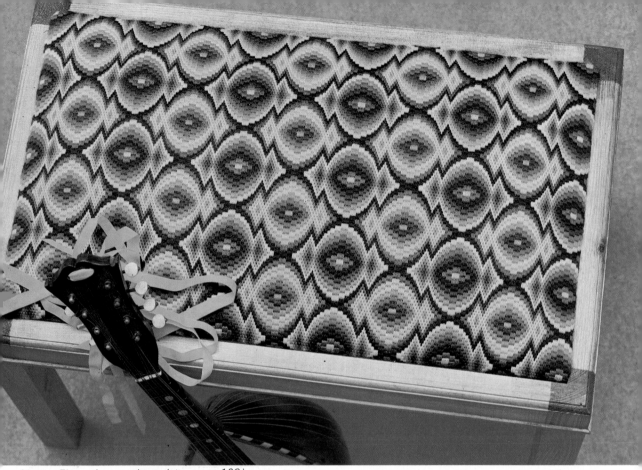

Above: Florentine stool top (see page 120).
Below: Norweave stool top (see opposite).

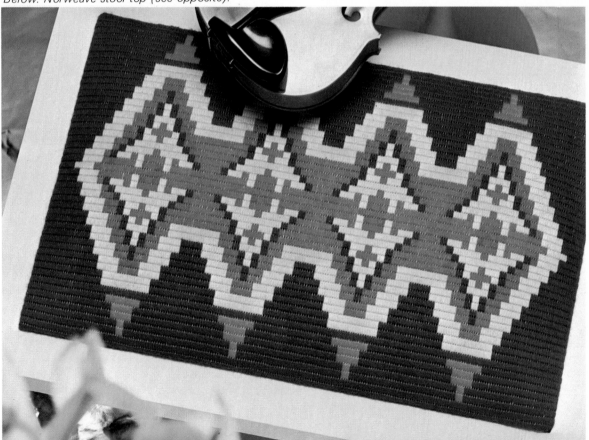

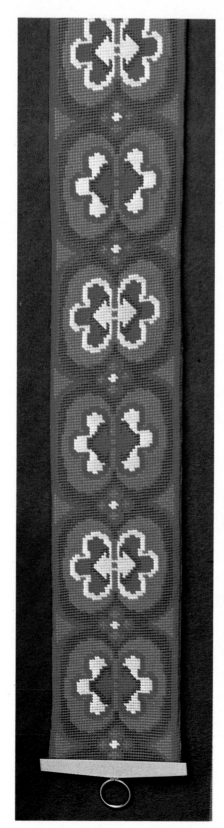

Left: bell pull (see page 114).
Above: head cushion (see page 112).

DIAGRAM A

fender stool top

Illustrated in colour on page 108.

MATERIALS
Of Coats Anchor Tapisserie Wool—20 skeins Flame 0332, 8 skeins Amber Gold 0308, 8 skeins Olive Green 0843, 7 skeins Black 0403, 4 skeins White 0402, and 2 skeins Canary Yellow 0288. $1\frac{1}{4}$yd. single thread tapestry canvas, 23in. wide, 18 threads to 1in. Stool with inset pad measuring 38in. by 14in. Milward 'Gold Seal' tapestry needle No. 19. Upholstery tacks.

MEASUREMENTS
Finished stool top measures 38in. by 14in.

STITCH
Satin (worked in blocks of 4 stitches each stitch worked over 4 threads of the canvas).

DIAGRAM
Diagram A gives one half of the design. Each background square on the diagram represents one block of 4 satin stitches over 4 threads of canvas.

TO MAKE
Mark the centre of canvas both ways with a line of basting stitches.

Prepare canvas, and mount it, if you are using a frame. Commence embroidery centrally, following colour key and diagram A. The blank arrows on the diagram mark the centre and should coincide with your basting stitches. Work the half of the design as given, for lower half of stool, then work upper half to correspond.

TO COMPLETE
Stretch canvas if necessary.
Place the embroidery centrally on the stool pad, right side uppermost. Fold the unworked border of canvas back and secure on underside of pad with upholstery tacks.

COLOUR KEY
Ⓞ Canary Yellow
☒ Amber Gold
• Flame
☐ White
■ Black
◉ Olive Green

DIAGRAM A

norweave picture

Illustrated in colour on page 89.

MATERIALS
Of Coats Anchor Tapisserie Wool—11 skeins White 0402, 3 skeins Peacock Blue (medium) 0168, 3 skeins Brown 0420, 2 skeins Cyclamen 086, 2 skeins Peacock Blue (dark) 0170, 2 skeins Olive Green (light) 0842, 2 skeins Olive Green (dark) 0843, 1 skein Apple Green 0204, and 1 skein Grass Green 0240. $\frac{1}{2}$yd. double thread tapestry canvas, 27in. wide, 10 holes to 1in. Piece of cardboard 21$\frac{1}{2}$in. by 13in. Mounting board 25in. by 17$\frac{1}{4}$in., with size of window in mount 20$\frac{1}{2}$in. by 12$\frac{1}{4}$in. Picture frame 25$\frac{1}{4}$in. by 17$\frac{1}{2}$in. (width of actual frame $\frac{1}{2}$in.). 2 picture rings. Milward 'Gold Seal' tapestry needle No. 19. Strong thread.

MEASUREMENTS
Finished embroidery measures approximately 13in. by 21$\frac{1}{2}$in.

STITCH
Satin (worked in blocks of 3 double stitches, each pair of stitches worked over 3 double threads of the canvas).

DIAGRAM
Diagram A gives the complete design. Each background square on the diagram represents one block of 3 double satin stitches worked over 3 double threads of the canvas.

TO MAKE
Mark the centre of canvas both ways with a line of basting stitches. Work stitches between a pair of narrow double threads. Prepare the canvas, and mount it, if you are using a frame. Commence the embroidery centrally, following colour key and diagram A. The blank arrows mark the centre and should coincide with your basting stitches.

TO COMPLETE
Stretch canvas if necessary.
Place the embroidery centrally over the cardboard, right side uppermost, fold the unworked border of canvas to the back and secure with pins inserted into the edge of the cardboard. Pin top edge first then pull firmly over the lower edge and pin in position. Repeat with side edges, pulling fabric until it lies taut on the cardboard.

Secure at the back by lacing side edges together with strong thread, then lacing top and bottom edges together. Remove pins. Mount centrally in mount (see page 64), and place in picture frame.

COLOUR KEY
- Cyclamen
- Medium Peacock Blue
- Dark Peacock Blue
- Apple Green
- Grass Green
- White
- Brown
- Light Olive Green
- Dark Olive Green

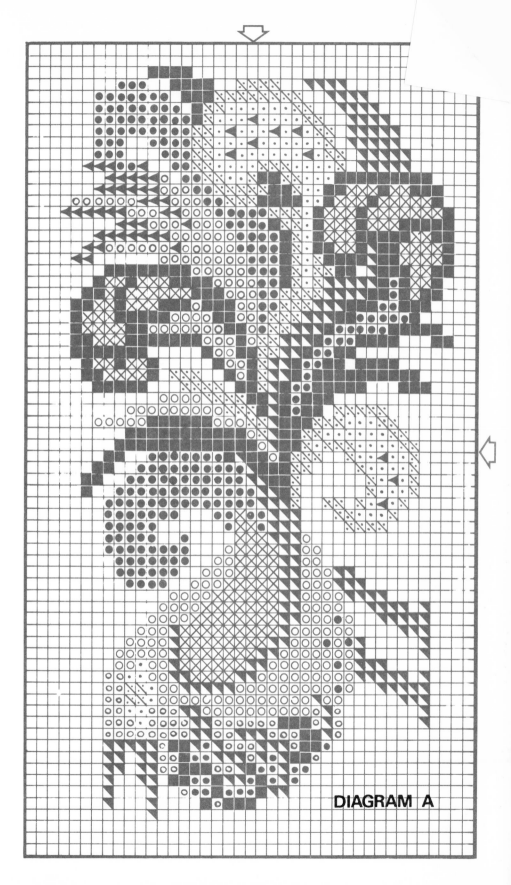

DIAGRAM A

bridal kneeler

Illustrated in colour on page 108.

MATERIALS

Of Coats Anchor Tapisserie Wool—44 skeins Saxe Blue 0145, 3 hanks or 17 skeins Cream 0386, 7 skeins Moss Green (medium) 0266, 7 skeins Cornflower Blue 0139, 5 skeins Beige 0376, 5 skeins Brown (dark) 0986, 4 skeins Moss Green (dark) 0269, 3 skeins Moss Green (light) 0264, and 3 skeins Brown (medium) 0984. $\frac{7}{8}$yd. double thread tapestry canvas, 44in. wide, 10 holes to 1in., or 1$\frac{3}{8}$yd. double thread canvas, 27 in. wide, 10 holes to 1in., Kneeler pad approximately 12$\frac{1}{4}$in. by 30$\frac{1}{4}$in. by 5$\frac{1}{4}$in. Piece of furnishing fabric to match Saxe Blue Tapisserie Wool, 15in. by 36in. for base. Milward 'Gold Seal' tapestry needle No. 19.

MEASUREMENTS

Finished kneeler measures approximately 12$\frac{1}{4}$in. by 30$\frac{1}{4}$in. by 5$\frac{1}{4}$in. deep.

DIAGRAM

Diagram A gives a little over half the design for the kneeler top. **Diagram B** (page 134) gives a little over half of one long side. **Diagram C** (page 134) gives one complete right-hand narrow side. Each of the background squares on the diagrams represents the double threads of the canvas.

STITCH

Trammed tent

TO MAKE

Mark the centre of the canvas both ways with a line of basting stitches. Mark out area embroidery will cover, also with basting stitches. Prepare and mount canvas in frame.

Commence embroidery centrally, following colour key and diagrams A, B and C. The blank arrows mark the centre, and these should coincide with your centre basting stitches.

Work the section of the design given in diagrams A, B and C first, then repeat in reverse. Work remaining long side in position, to correspond with long side already worked.

Note. When a 27in. canvas is used, this design should be turned so it is placed centrally on the piece of canvas with the narrow end between the 2 selvedges.

COLOUR KEY

- ◪ Cornflower Blue
- ☐ Saxe Blue
- ⊙ Light Moss Green
- ⊠ Medium Moss Green
- ● Dark Moss Green
- ⫽ Beige
- ⁄ Cream
- ⋀ Medium Brown
- ◤ Dark Brown

TO COMPLETE

Stretch canvas if necessary.

Trim canvas and make up into kneeler, following instructions beginning on page 88.

DIAGRAM A

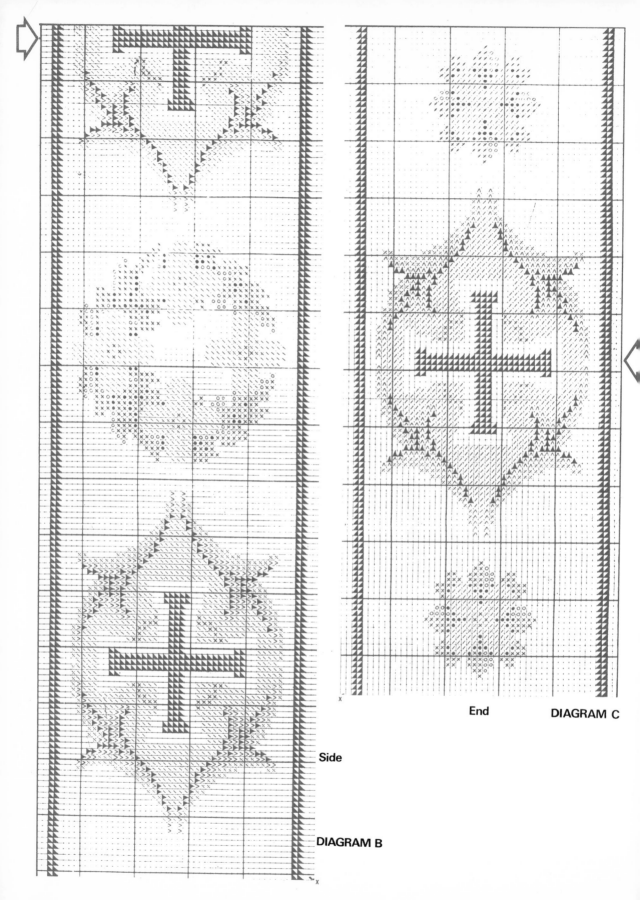

Side

DIAGRAM B

End

DIAGRAM C

york kneeler

Illustrated in colour on page 144.

MATERIALS

Of Coats Anchor Tapisserie Wool — 24 skeins Kingfisher (medium) 0162, 7 skeins Kingfisher (dark) 0164, 4 skeins 0311 Tangerine, 1 skein Kingfisher (light) 0158, and 1 skein Amber Gold 0309. ¾yd. double thread tapestry canvas, 27in. wide, 10 holes to 1in. Milward 'Gold Seal' tapestry needle No. 19. Kneeler pad approximately 11in. by 15in. by 3in. Piece of furnishing fabric to match background colour of embroidery, 13in. by 17in., for base.

MEASUREMENTS

Finished kneeler measures approximately 11in. by 15in. by 3in. deep.

DIAGRAM (see pages 136 and 137).

Diagram A gives the complete design for top of kneeler and one complete long side and one complete short side. Each background square on the diagram represents the double threads of the canvas. (**Note.** This diagram has been separated into two sections. Both sections should have centre edges placed together to give complete diagram A.)

TO MAKE

Mark centre of canvas both ways with basting stitches. Mark out area embroidery will cover, remembering to add 2nd long side and 2nd short side, also with basting stitches. Prepare and mount canvas in frame.

Work embroidery, following colour key and diagram A. The blank arrows mark the centre and should coincide with your centre basting stitches. Commence the embroidery centrally and work the top and 2 side sections as given. Work remaining side sections to correspond.

TO COMPLETE

Trim canvas and make up into kneeler, following instructions beginning on page 88.

STITCH

Trammed tent

COLOUR KEY

- ○ Light Kingfisher
- Medium Kingfisher
- ◤ Dark Kingfisher
- ∴ Amber Gold
- ╱ Tangerine

DIAGRAM A

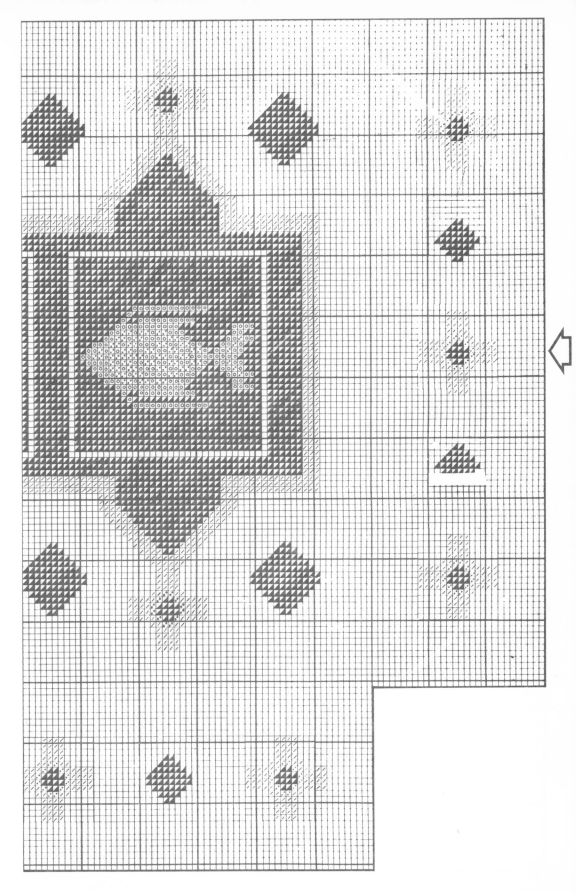

137

ely kneeler

Illustrated in colour on page 144.

MATERIALS

Of Coats Anchor Tapisserie Wool—3 hanks or 14 skeins Moss Green 0269, 8 skeins Jade 0185, 7 skeins Maroon 0873, 6 skeins Ecru 0390, and 5 skeins Muscat Green 0281. $\frac{7}{8}$yd. double thread tapestry canvas, 36in. wide, 10 holes to 1in., or 1yd. double thread tapestry canvas, 27in. wide, 10 holes to 1in. Kneeler pad approximately 12in. by 15in. by 5$\frac{1}{2}$in. Piece of furnishing fabric to match one of thread shades, 14in. by 17in., for base. Milward 'Gold Seal' tapestry needle No. 19.

MEASUREMENTS

Finished kneeler measures approximately 12in. by 15in. by 5$\frac{1}{2}$in. deep.

DIAGRAM

Diagram A gives the designs for motifs A and B for top of kneeler. Each background square on the diagram represents the double threads of the canvas.
Diagram B (page 140) gives half of one long side.
Diagram C (page 140) gives a guide to the position of the motifs on top of the kneeler.

TO MAKE

Mark centre of canvas both ways with basting stitches. Mark out area embroidery will cover, remembering to add 2nd long side and 2nd short side, also with basting stitches. Prepare and mount canvas in frame.

Work embroidery, following colour key and the diagrams. The blank arrows mark the centre and should coincide with your centre basting stitches. Work 'IHS' motifs first working motifs A and B where indicated on diagram. All background areas are worked in Ecru. Work half of one long side as given on diagram B, then repeat in reverse to complete side. In a similar way work one short side, working bracketed section on diagram B only. Work remaining sides to correspond.

Note. When a 27in. canvas is used, this design should be turned so it is placed centrally on the piece of canvas with the narrow end between the 2 selvedges.

TO COMPLETE

Stretch canvas if necessary.
Trim canvas and make up into kneeler, following instructions beginning on page 88.

STITCH
Trammed tent

COLOUR KEY
◩ Moss Green
◯ Jade
☐ Maroon
◪ Ecru
☒ Muscat Green

138

DIAGRAM A

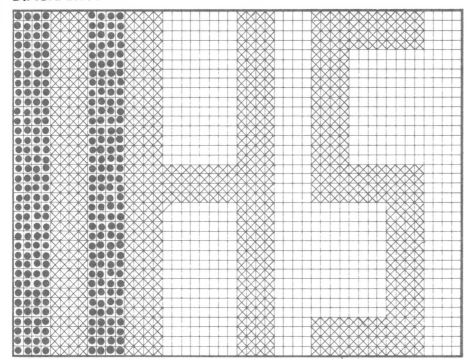

Motif A

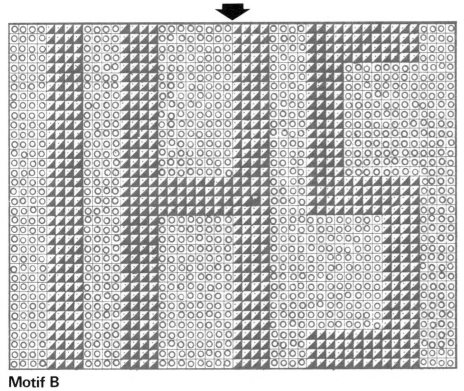

Motif B

DIAGRAM B   (section of side)

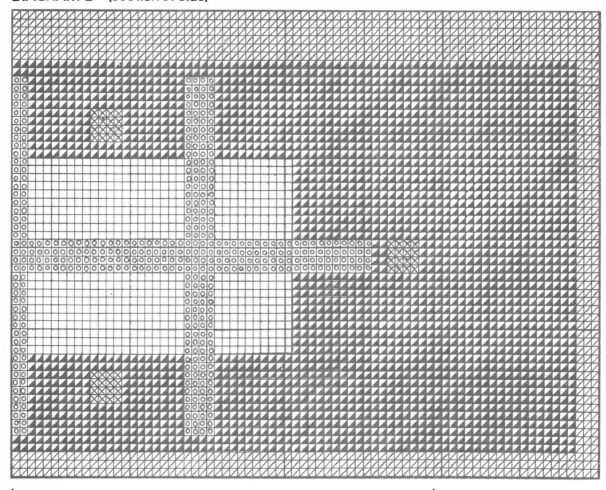

short side stops here

DIAGRAM C

A	B	A
B	A	B
A	B	A

beaded pincushion

MATERIALS
Of stranded cotton—a skein each in 3 shades of red, pink and orange. Piece of single thread tapestry canvas, 12in. by 12in., 16 threads to 1in. Piece of backing fabric to match one of thread colours, 3¼in. by 3¾in. Oddment of pink felt. Few small orange beads. Oddment (about 2in.) of orange raffia. Pad measuring approximately 2¾in. by 2¼in. by 1½in. deep. Tapestry needle No. 20.

MEASUREMENTS
Finished pincushion measures 2¾in. by 2¼in. by 1½in. deep.

DIAGRAMS
Diagram A (page 145) gives the design for the top, one long side and one short side with the various stitches, the felt appliqué raffia and beads all indicated. The background lines on the diagram represent the threads of the canvas.
Diagram B (page 142) gives a guide to the thread colours used throughout the design.

STITCHES
Tent
Satin
Fern
Hungarian
Flat
Florentine

TO MAKE

Note. Use 4 strands throughout.

Mark the centre of canvas both ways with a line of basting stitches. Mark out the area the embroidery will cover also with a line of basting stitches. Prepare canvas, and mount it, if you are using a frame.

Trim the felt oddment to a strip measuring 1in. by $\frac{1}{4}$in. Stitch it in position to canvas, following diagram A. Roll up raffia to a flat coil and stitch it in place, pulling out 'corners' so it forms a square shape on canvas. Stitch beads in position. Now work embroidery, following stitch key and diagram A for position of stitches, and colour key and diagram B for thread colours. The blank arrows on diagram A mark the centre, and should coincide with your centre basting stitches. Work remaining long and short sides to correspond.

TO COMPLETE

Stretch canvas if necessary. Trim to within 1in. of embroidery. Stitch corners together, right sides facing and stitching close to the embroidery. Turn right side out and insert pad. Fold unworked border of canvas round lower edge on to base of pad and lace to secure. Turn in $\frac{1}{2}$in. hem round all edges of backing fabric. Place in position on base of pincushion, wrong sides together, and oversew neatly round the edges.

COLOUR KEY

1 Light Red
2 Medium Red
3 Dark Red
4 Orange
5 Pink

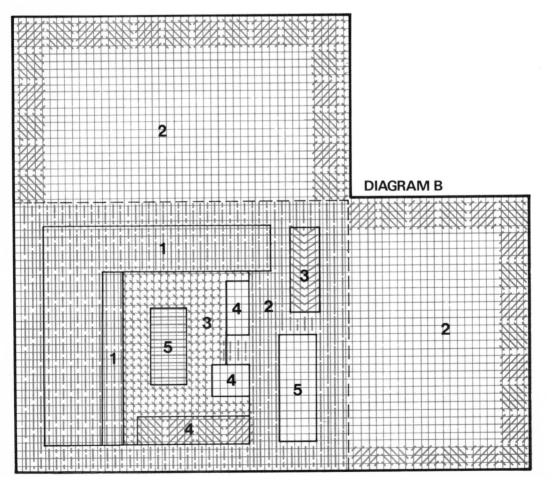

DIAGRAM B

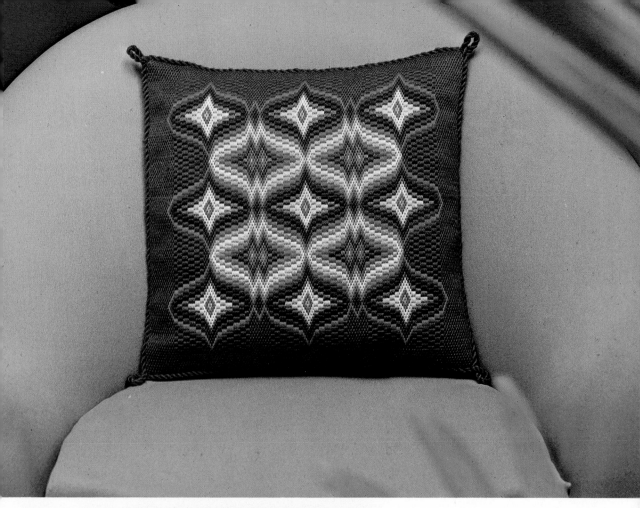

Above: Florentine cushion (see page 166).
Left: traditional chair seat (see page 168).

Above: Ely kneeler (see page 138).
Right: York kneeler (see page 135).

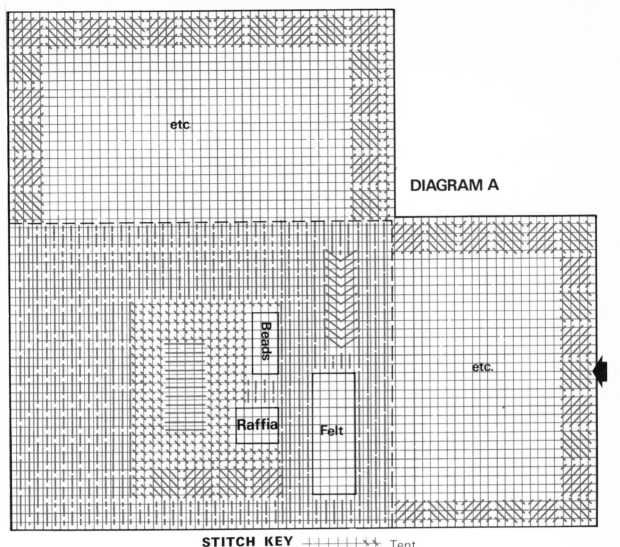

DIAGRAM A

etc.

Beads

Raffia

Felt

etc.

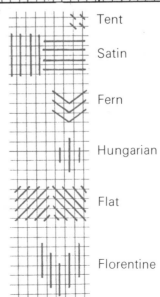

STITCH KEY

	Tent
	Satin
	Fern
	Hungarian
	Flat
	Florentine

owl picture

Illustrated in colour on page 72.

MATERIALS

Of stranded cotton—8 skeins deep turquoise, 1 skein each of dark, medium and light brown, beige, cream, orange and black. Piece of single thread tapestry canvas, $12\frac{1}{4}$in. by $13\frac{1}{2}$in., 18 threads to 1in. Approximately 30in. dark brown rug wool. Piece of cardboard, approximately $6\frac{1}{4}$in. by $7\frac{1}{2}$in. Piece of carboard covered with brown hessian (burlap), 12in. by 15in. (optional). Tapestry needle No. 20. Strong thread for lacing.

MEASUREMENTS

Finished owl picture, excluding mounting (if used), is approximately $6\frac{1}{4}$in. by $7\frac{1}{2}$in.

DIAGRAMS

Diagram A gives the complete design with the position of the various stitches indicated. The background lines on the diagram represent the threads of the canvas.
Diagram B (page 148) gives a guide to the thread colours used throughout the design.

TO MAKE

Note. Use 6 strands throughout.
Mark the centre of canvas both ways with basting stitches. Prepare canvas, and mount it, if you are using a frame. Work embroidery, following stitch key (page 148) and diagram A for stitches, and colour key and diagram B for thread colours. The blank arrows on diagram A mark the centre and should coincide with your basting stitches.

The background is worked in a variation of Jacquard stitch— follow diagram A for lengths of stitches. Outline owl's beak with back stitches worked in black.

TO COMPLETE

Stretch canvas, if necessary.
Place canvas centrally over cardboard. Fold unworked border of canvas to the wrong side and secure with pins inserted into the edge of the cardboard. Pin the top edge first, then pull firmly over the lower edge and pin in position. Repeat with side edges, pulling fabric until it lies taut on the cardboard. Secure at the back by lacing with strong thread: lace top and bottom edges together, then lace side edges together in a similar way. Remove pins. Mount centrally on hessian-covered cardboard (if used). Outline owl picture with length of rug wool, stitched neatly in position.

STITCHES

Florentine
Fern
Rice
Hungarian
Gobelin
Tent
Eyelet
Jacquard variation

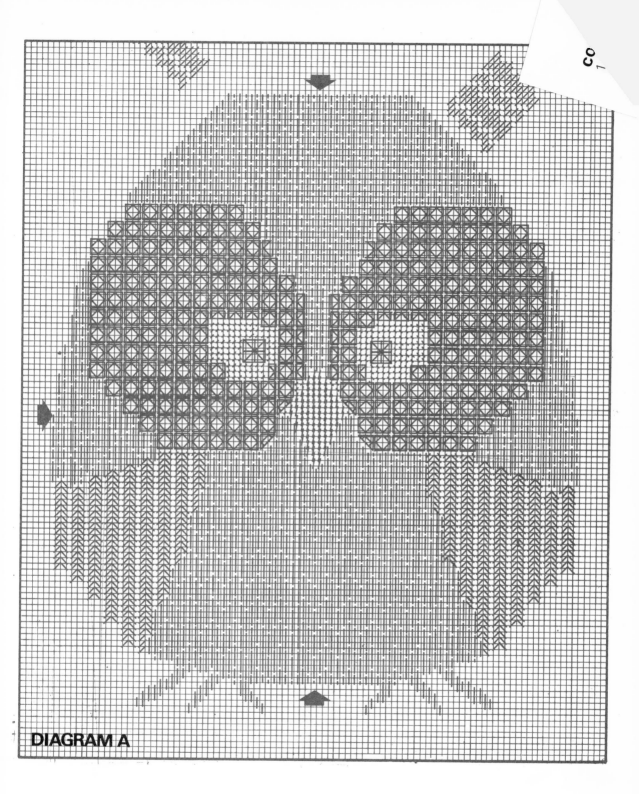

DIAGRAM A

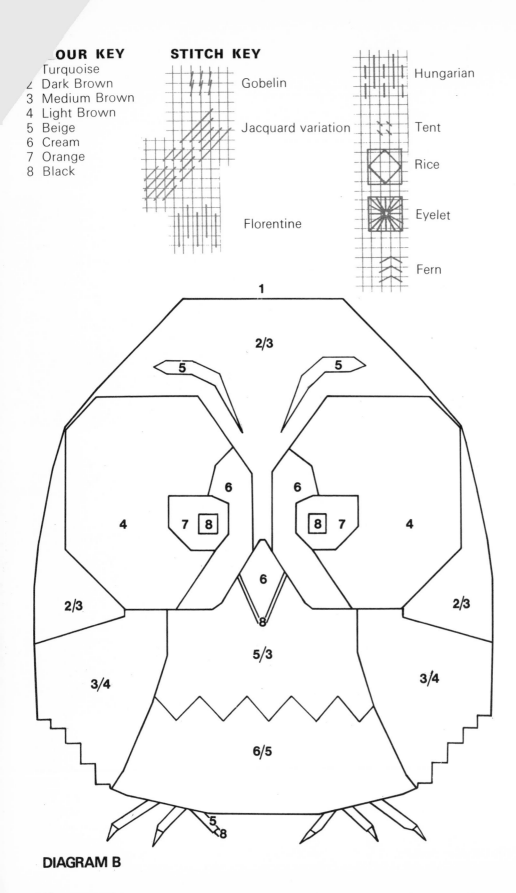

COLOUR KEY

1 Turquoise
2 Dark Brown
3 Medium Brown
4 Light Brown
5 Beige
6 Cream
7 Orange
8 Black

STITCH KEY

Gobelin

Jacquard variation

Florentine

Hungarian

Tent

Rice

Eyelet

Fern

DIAGRAM B

square pincushion

MATERIALS
Of crewel wool—1 skein each of dark, medium and pale green, and dark, medium and pale pink. Two 10in. squares of single thread tapestry canvas, 16 threads to 1in. Pad or suitable firm stuffing to measure approximately 3in. square. Tapestry needle No. 20.

MEASUREMENTS
Finished pincushion measures approximately 4in. square.

DIAGRAMS
Diagram A shows the complete design for each side of the pincushion (if wished both sides may be made alike), with the position of the various stitches indicated. The background lines on the diagrams represent the threads of the canvas.
Diagram B gives a guide to the colours used throughout the design.

TO MAKE
Note. Each side of the pincushion should be made separately. Mark the centre of each canvas square both ways with basting stitches. Prepare canvas, and mount it, if you are using a frame.

Work embroidery, following stitch key and diagram A for position of stitches, and colour key and diagram B for the thread colours. The blank arrows on the diagrams mark the centre and should coincide with your basting stitches.

TO COMPLETE
Stretch canvas if necessary. Trim canvas to within 1in. of embroidery. Fold back unworked canvas edges on both sections, but leave a border of 4 threads of the canvas. Place both embroidery sections together, wrong sides facing. Using medium green wool, work long-armed cross stitches round 3 sides, over the 4-thread border of canvas, and so linking the 2 sections together. Insert pad, and close the remaining side with another row of long-armed cross stitches in medium green.

STITCHES

Flat	Cross
Long-armed cross	Double straight cross
Rice	Eye
Tent	Plaited
Satin	Italian cross

STITCH KEY

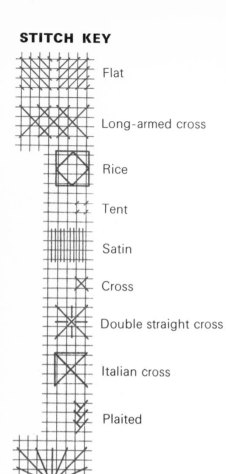

Flat

Long-armed cross

Rice

Tent

Satin

Cross

Double straight cross

Italian cross

Plaited

Eye

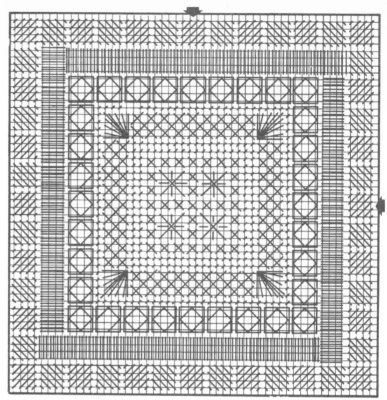

DIAGRAM A 1st side

COLOUR KEY
1 Light Green
2 Medium Green
3 Dark Green
4 Light Pink
5 Medium Pink
6 Dark Pink

Note. Rice stitches marked 5/4 are worked with medium pink as the basic cross, light pink for diagonal corner stitches.

DIAGRAM A 2nd side

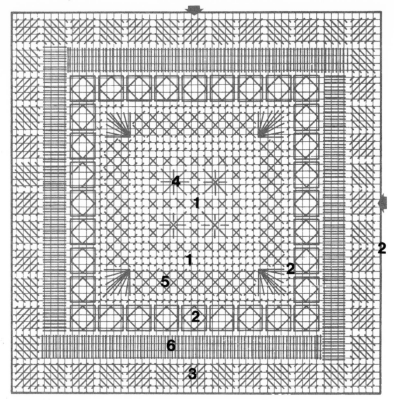

DIAGRAM B

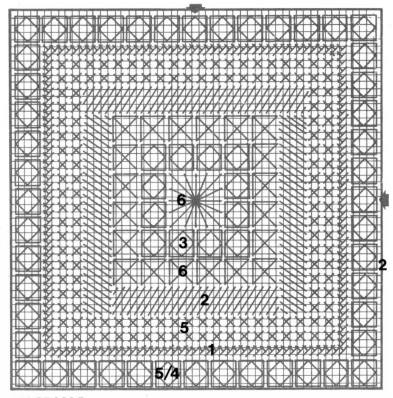

DIAGRAM B

cat pincushion

STITCHES
Chequer
Gobelin
Flat
Brick
Cross
Tent
Long-armed cross

MATERIALS
Of stranded cotton—6 skeins medium grey, 1 skein each of dark brown, medium brown and cream, short length of blue. Piece of single thread tapestry canvas, $12\frac{1}{2}$in. by $11\frac{1}{2}$in., 18 threads to 1in. Pad measuring approximately $3\frac{1}{4}$in. by $2\frac{3}{4}$in. by $1\frac{1}{4}$in. deep. Piece of grey backing material, $4\frac{1}{4}$in. by $3\frac{3}{4}$in. Tapestry needle No. 20.

MEASUREMENTS
Finished pincushion measures approximately $3\frac{1}{4}$in. by $2\frac{3}{4}$in. by $1\frac{1}{4}$in. deep.

DIAGRAMS
Diagram A gives the design for top, one long and one short side, with the position of the various stitches. The background lines on the diagram represent the threads of the canvas.
Diagram B gives a guide to the thread colours used throughout the design.

TO MAKE
Note. Use 6 strands throughout.
Mark the centre of canvas both ways with basting stitches. Prepare canvas and mount it, if you are using a frame. Work the embroidery, following the stitch key and diagram A for position of stitches, and colour key and diagram B for thread colours. The blank arrows on diagram A mark the centre and should coincide with your basting stitches.
   The background for top design is worked in a variation of chequer stitch. The sides are worked in long-armed cross. Work remaining long and short sides to correspond.

TO COMPLETE
Stretch canvas if necessary. Trim to within 1in. of embroidery. Stitch corners together, right sides facing, and stitching close to the embroidery. Turn right side out and insert pad. Fold unworked border of canvas round lower edge on to base of pad and baste to secure. Turn in $\frac{1}{2}$in. hem round all edges of backing fabric. Place in position on base of pincushion, and oversew neatly round the edges to secure.

STITCH KEY

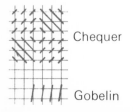

Chequer

Gobelin

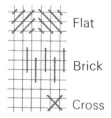

Flat

Brick

Cross

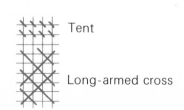

Tent

Long-armed cross

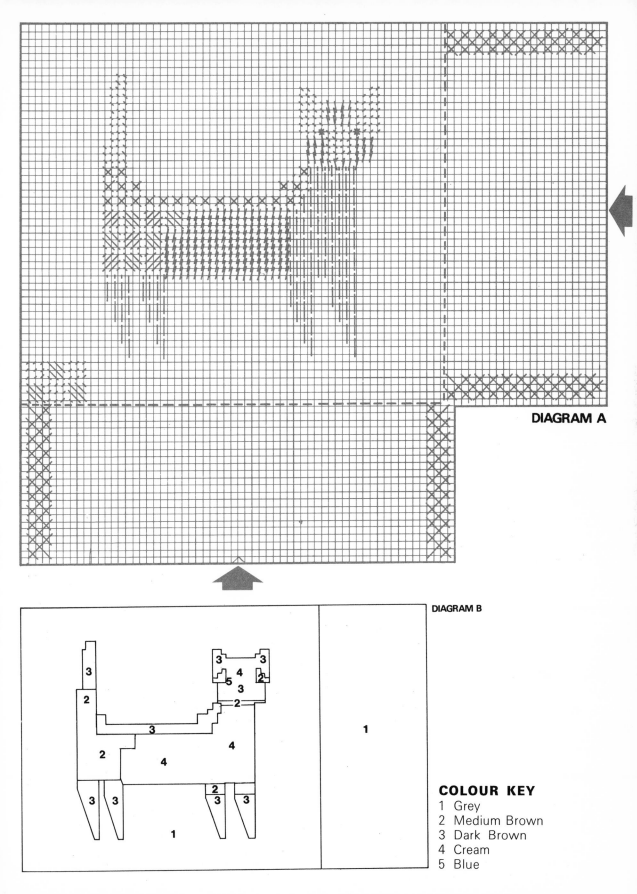

DIAGRAM A

DIAGRAM B

COLOUR KEY
1 Grey
2 Medium Brown
3 Dark Brown
4 Cream
5 Blue

153

butterfly paperweight

MATERIALS

Of stranded cotton—1 skein each of light brown, tan and turquoise. A 9in. square of single thread tapestry canvas, 14 threads to 1in. Piece of leather, 8in. by 5in. Oddment of turquoise leather for butterfly (approximately 1in. by 2in.). A 2in. length of iron piping, 2in. in diameter. Oddments of polythene sheeting and cotton flannelette. Tapestry needle No. 17. Fabric glue. Approximately 8in. thin brown cord.

MEASUREMENTS

Finished paperweight measures approximately $2\frac{1}{2}$in. across, 2in. deep.

DIAGRAMS

Diagram A gives the complete canvas design for top of paperweight with the position of the various stitches. The background lines on the diagram represent the threads of the canvas.
Diagram B gives a guide to the thread colours used throughout the design.

TO MAKE

Note. Use 6 strands throughout.
Mark the centre of the canvas with basting stitches both ways. Prepare canvas, and mount it, if you are using a frame. Work the embroidery, following the stitch key and diagram A for position of stitches, and colour key and diagram B for thread colours. The blank arrows on diagram A mark the centre and should coincide with your basting stitches.

TO COMPLETE

Stretch canvas, if necessary. Trim canvas to within 1in. of embroidery.

Cut out a butterfly shape from leather and sew it to the centre of embroidery with satin stitches in light brown. If wished, work a few decorative embroidery stitches on the butterfly before sewing to canvas work.

Cover iron piping with several layers of polythene, then with 2 thicknesses of cotton flannelette. Bind tightly with strong thread to hold in position. The finished 'weight' should have a top circumference exactly the same size as actual embroidery.

Place embroidery on top of weight, right side uppermost. Fold unworked border of canvas down on to sides of weight, and secure with a spot of fabric glue. Cut a piece of leather to fit exactly round the side, and another piece for the base. Stick the side piece, butting the edges exactly and securing with a little fabric glue. Sew the base by hand to the sides. Place cord round edge of top and secure with a spot of fabric glue.

STITCHES

Tent
Satin
Double straight cross
Oblong cross

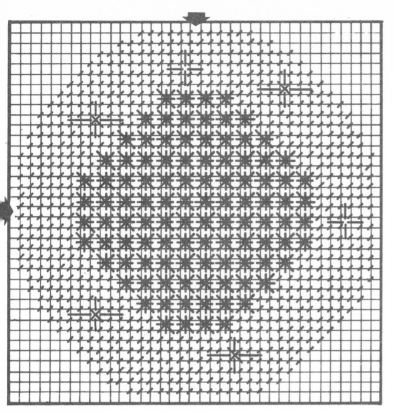

DIAGRAM A

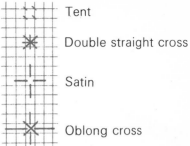
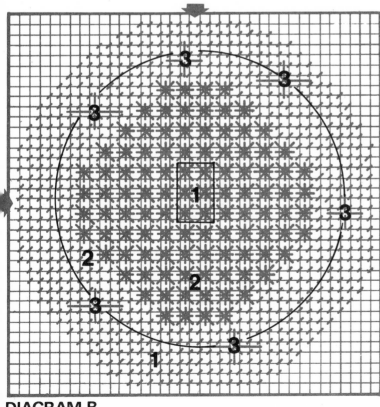

DIAGRAM B

COLOUR KEY
1 Light Brown
2 Tan
3 Turquoise

rug wool and felt cushion

MATERIALS

4 oz. rug wool in tan, 1 oz. thick knit wool in turquoise. $\frac{1}{2}$ yd. rug canvas, 22 in. wide, 4 threads to 1 in. Piece of furnishing fabric, 14 in. by 17 in., to match or contrast with embroidery thread colours. $\frac{1}{3}$ yd. felt in turquoise, 36 in. wide. Tapestry needle No. 13. A cushion pad, approximately 13 in. by 16 in.

MEASUREMENTS

Finished cushion measures approximately 13 in. by 16 in.

DIAGRAMS

Diagram A shows the complete design, with the positions of the various stitches, and of the felt appliqués. This diagram also indicates the thread colours used. The background lines on the diagram represent the threads of the canvas.

TO MAKE

Mark the centre of canvas both ways with basting stitches. Prepare canvas and mount, if you are using a frame.

Cut 5 pieces of felt, each 2 in. by 7 in. Shape one end of each strip to a point. Now cut 15 strips of felt, each 1$\frac{3}{4}$ in. by 6$\frac{3}{4}$ in. Point one end of each of these strips, in a similar way as for bigger strips.

On each position marked on diagram A for a felt appliqué, place 3 small strips, and top each with 1 big strip (the smaller strips act as padding and prevent the marks of the canvas mesh showing through). It is also a good idea to trim edges of two of the small strips so the three strips are of a graduated size— place smallest strip next to canvas, then the middle size, then the largest.

Sew felt in position with stab stitches through felt and canvas. Now work embroidery, following stitch and colour key and diagram A. The blank arrows on the diagram mark the centre and should coincide with your basting stitches.

Work stitches in direction indicated on the diagram. Rice stitches are worked with tan rug wool for basic cross, turquoise thick knit wool for corner diagonal stitches.

TO COMPLETE

Couch 4 strands of thick knit wool round each felt shape.

Stretch canvas if necessary. Trim to within 1 in of embroidery. Place embroidery and backing fabric together, right sides facing, and stitch round 2 long sides and 1 short side, stitching close to the embroidery. Turn cover right side out, insert cushion pad, turn in seam allowance along remaining open edge, and slipstitch neatly.

STITCHES

Reversed tent
Rice

STITCH AND COLOUR KEY

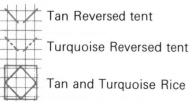

Tan Reversed tent

Turquoise Reversed tent

Tan and Turquoise Rice

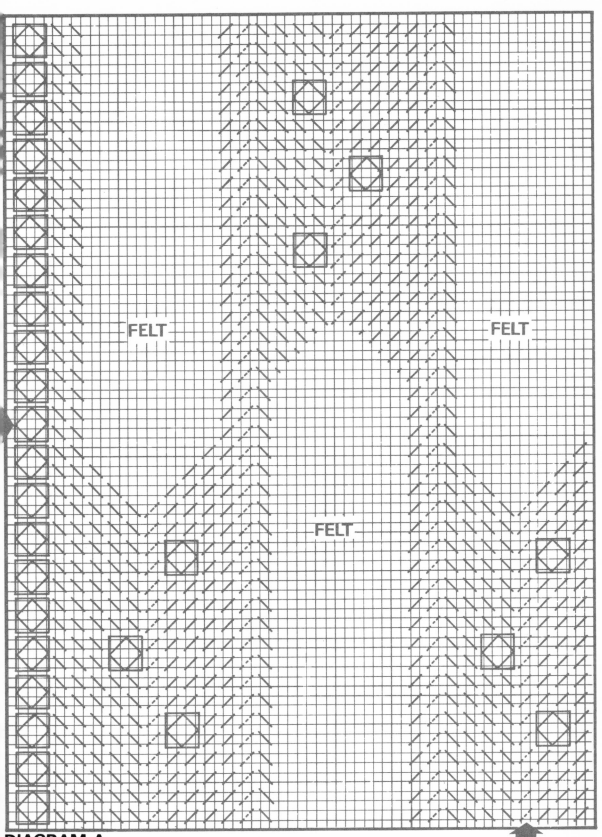

FELT   FELT

FELT

DIAGRAM A

157

belt

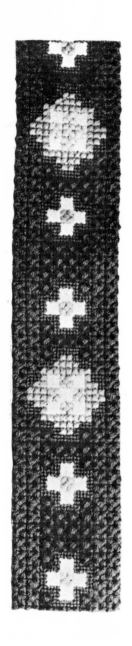

MATERIALS
2oz. dark blue crewel wool (for background), 1 skein each of white, green and orange tapisserie wool, 1 skein white stranded green and orange tapisserie wool, 1 skein white stranded cotton (for diagonal stitches on rice stitches—use 12 strands). 1yd. single thread tapestry canvas, 6in. wide, 12 threads to 1in. 4 hooks and eyes to fasten. Tapestry needle No. 17. Piece of backing fabric in a colour to match or contrast with embroidery threads, to fit finished belt size plus $\frac{1}{2}$in. seam allowance on all edges (petersham ribbon would be suitable).

MEASUREMENTS
Finished belt is $2\frac{3}{4}$in. wide, and can be made as long as required to fit waist size.

DIAGRAMS
Diagram A gives a section of the design with the position of the stitches. This section is repeated until belt is required length. The background lines on the diagram represent the threads of the canvas.
Diagram B gives a guide to the thread colours used.

TO MAKE
Mark centre of canvas lengthwise with basting stitches. Prepare canvas.

Work embroidery, following stitch key and diagram A for position of stitches, and colour key and diagram B for thread colours. The blank arrow on diagram A marks the centre and should coincide with your basting stitches. Continue to work repeats of the design as given until belt is the required length.

TO COMPLETE
Stretch canvas if necessary. Trim canvas to within 1in. of embroidery at either end, but leave side borders as they are. Press canvas borders to back of belt and baste to hold in position. Turn in $\frac{1}{2}$in. seam allowance round edges of fabric backing strip and place on embroidered strip, wrong sides together. Oversew neatly round edges.

Sew hooks and eyes to narrow ends of belt to fasten.

STITCHES
Rice
Tent
Cross

DIAGRAM A

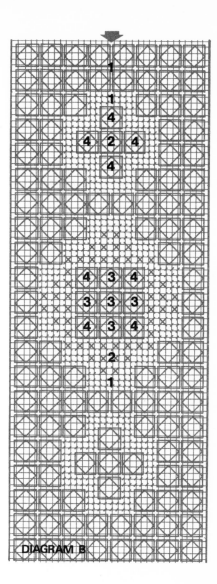

DIAGRAM B

STITCH KEY

Rice

Tent

Cross

COLOUR KEY
1 Dark Blue
2 Orange
3 Green
4 White

Note. Rice stitches in white have the basic cross worked in white tapisserie wool, diagonal stitches are worked in white stranded cotton (use 12 strands).

florentine
spectacle case

MATERIALS
Of stranded cotton—2 skeins each of grey, pale lilac, dark lilac, pale blue, tan and dark brown. Piece of single thread tapestry canvas, $22\frac{1}{2}$in. by $9\frac{1}{2}$in., 14 threads to 1in. Piece of lining 18in. by $5\frac{1}{2}$in. $\frac{3}{4}$yd. dark lilac cord. Tapestry needle No. 20. Two press fasteners. Mediumweight interfacing (optional).

MEASUREMENTS
Finished spectacle case measures 7in. by $3\frac{1}{2}$in.

STITCH
Florentine (worked over 4 vertical threads).

DIAGRAM
Diagram A gives a section of the design. The background lines on the diagram represent the threads of the canvas.

TO MAKE
Note. Use 12 strands of cotton throughout.
Mark centre of canvas lengthwise with basting stitches. Prepare canvas, and mount, if you are using a frame. Starting at the top, work section of embroidery as given on diagram A, following colour key. Step stitches down or up as indicated on diagram. The blank arrow on the diagram marks the centre and should coincide with your basting stitches. Continue to work section of design within brackets until work is 16in (or length required).

TO COMPLETE
Stretch canvas, if required. Trim canvas to within 1in. of embroidery. Cut lining to same shape and size as canvas strip. Turn in seam allowance on lining, and unworked border on canvas and place together, wrong sides facing, oversew neatly round edges. Fold strip widthwise 6½in. from straight end, and slip stitch side sides together, leaving ½in. unstitched at top of each seam. Fold down remaining section of strip to form flap. Stitch press studs in position to fasten. (If wished, interfacing can be sandwiched between embroidery and lining to give further stiffening.)

Sew cord edges and down side seams.

COLOUR KEY
1 Dark Lilac
2 Pale Blue
3 Tan
4 Dark Brown
5 Grey
6 Pale Lilac

DIAGRAM A

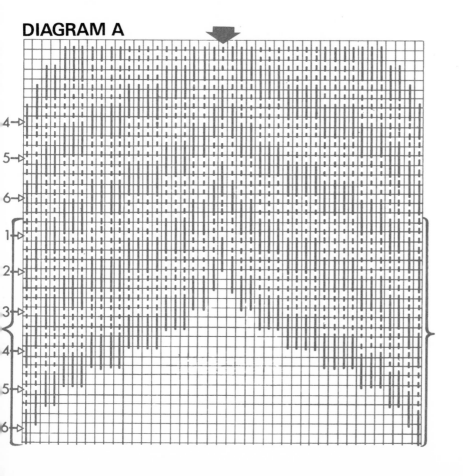

three cat cushion

Illustrated in colour on page 89.

MATERIALS

2oz hard-wearing double knitting wool in dark blue (for background), of stranded cotton—1 skein each of cream, gold, orange, yellow, green, grey and black (for faces), a variety of embroidery and knitting wools in white, and shades of yellow, orange, brown and grey (for remainder of embroidery). Piece of raffia canvas, 14in. by 18in., 10 threads to 1in. $\frac{1}{2}$yd. furnishing velvet or other suitable fabric in dark blue, 48in. wide. A cushion pad, 12in. by 16in. Tapestry needle No. 17.

MEASUREMENTS

Finished cushion measures 12in. by 16in. Embroidered panel measures 12in. by 8in.

DIAGRAMS

Diagram A gives the design for cats with the position of the various stitches. The background lines on the diagram represent the threads of the canvas.

Diagram B (see page 164) gives a guide to the thread colours used throughout the design.

Diagram C (see page 164) shows knotted cable chain stitch: work from right to left. Bring thread through at A and place it along the line of the design, then, with the thread under the needle, take a stitch at B, pass the needle under the stitch between A and B without piercing the fabric (as shown at C). With the thread under the needle, take slanting stitch across the line at D, close to the knot just formed. Pull the thread through and continue in this way along line of work.

STITCHES

Flat stitch (in an elongated form—used as background, to complement the rectangular shape of the panel)
Tent
Rice
Flat
Mosaic
Brick
Parisian
Ray
Fern
Cross
Knotted cable chain

TO MAKE

Note. This design shows a natural form being reduced to simple geometric shapes.

Use 12 strands of stranded cotton throughout. Mark the centre of canvas both ways with basting stitches. Prepare canvas, and mount it, if you are using a frame. Work embroidery, following stitch key and diagram A for position of stitches, and colour key and diagram B for thread colours. The blank arrows mark the centre and should coincide with your basting stitches. Flat stitch used for the background consists of 6 individual stitches and is worked as follows: work stitches in turn over 1 intersection of the canvas threads, then over 2, then over 3, work another stitch over the same 3 vertical threads but drop to the intersections below, then continue in the usual way working first over 2 intersections, then finally over 1 intersection.

TO COMPLETE

Stretch canvas if necessary. Trim to within 1in. of embroidery.

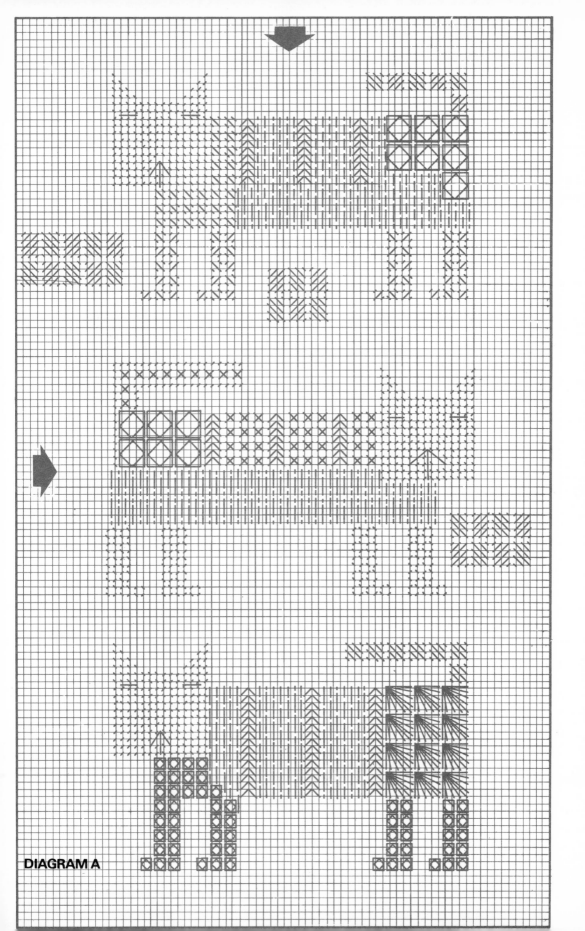

DIAGRAM A

DIAGRAM C

Cut fabric into 2 pieces, each 5½in. by 14in. (for side panels), cut one piece 18in. by 14in. (for back of cushion).

With right sides facing, stitch each side edge of embroidered panel to one fabric side panel, lining up edges and stitching close to the embroidery.

When both side panels are stitched in position lay whole section flat and work a vertical row of knotted cable chain stitch on either side of centre panel. Use dark blue wool to match background of embroidery, and work line of stitches about ¼in. from the embroidered panel.

Place back and front of cushion together, right sides facing, and taking 1in. turnings, stitch round 2 long sides and one short side. Turn right side out, insert cushion pad, and turn in 1in. seam allowance along remaining short side. Slipstitch neatly together.

STITCH KEY

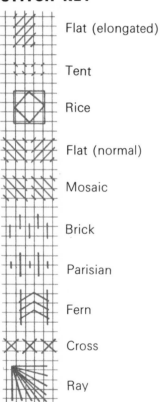

Flat (elongated)

Tent

Rice

Flat (normal)

Mosaic

Brick

Parisian

Fern

Cross

Ray

COLOUR KEY

1	Dark Blue	7	Light Brown
2	White	8	Dark Brown
3	Cream	9	Grey
4	Gold	10	Green
5	Orange	11	Black
6	Dark Gold		

Note. Where 2 numbers are given together on Diagram B, these stitches are worked in a combination of the 2 colours indicated.

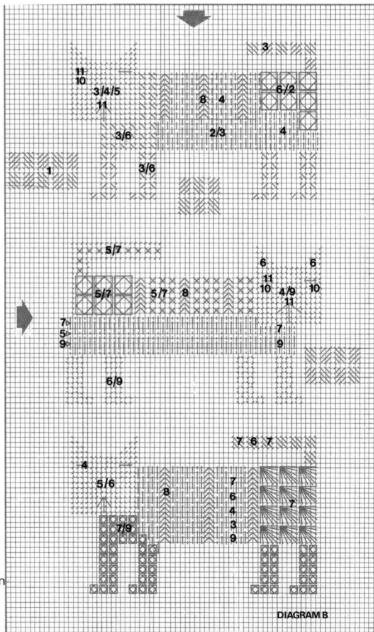

DIAGRAM B

164

inset panel bag

MATERIALS
1oz. scarlet double knitting wool, oddments of white and black double knitting or tapisserie wool and oddments of white raffia. Piece of single thread raffia canvas, 14in. by 15in., 10 threads to 1in. ½yd. plastic-coated cotton, 36in. wide. ½yd. lining fabric, 36in. wide. Two 1in. rings. A press fastener. Tapestry needle No. 17.

MEASUREMENTS
Finished bag measures approximately 11in. by 9in. Canvas panel measures 8in. by 9in.

DIAGRAM (see page 166)
Diagram A gives the complete design with the position of the various stitches indicated. The background lines on the diagram represent the threads of the canvas. Turn diagram sideways.

TO MAKE
Mark the centre of canvas both ways with basting stitches. Prepare canvas, and mount it, if you are using a frame. Work embroidery, following stitch key and diagram A for position of stitches. The blank arrows on diagram mark the centre and should coincide with your basting stitches. This design is rather like a sampler in that it consists of different areas of stitches. If preferred, different stitches can be substituted for the ones shown. Except where indicated on the stitch and colour key, the design is worked throughout in red.

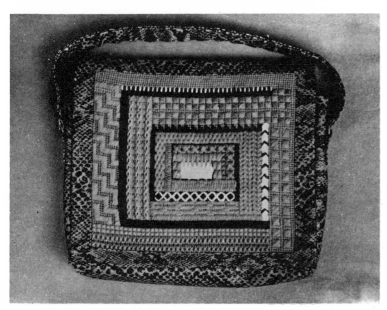

STITCHES
Tent
Satin
Flat
Byzantine
Shell
Oblong cross
Hungarian
Rice
Knotted
Greek
Fern
Scottish
Long-armed cross
Cross

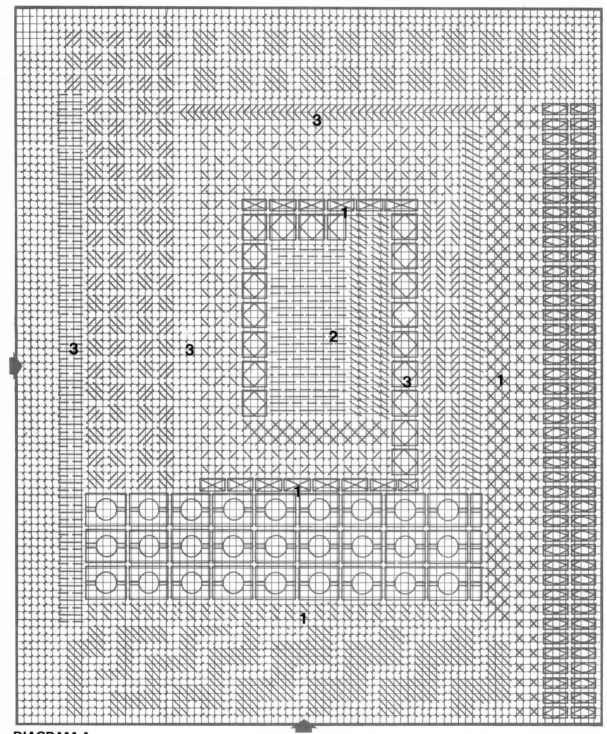

DIAGRAM A

Note. Turn diagram sideways to work embroidery.

TO COMPLETE

Stretch canvas, if necessary. Trim to within 1 in. of embroidery.

From plastic-coated cotton cut one piece 31 in. by 13 in. for main section of bag; cut 2 strips each 4 in. by 10 in. for side gussets; cut 2 strips each 21 in. by 2 in. for handle. Following instructions on page 67 stitch canvas panel in place to main bag section. Position panel 1¾ in. from one narrow end, and 2 in. from each side edge.

Lay strip flat, right side down, clip into corners then press 1 in. seam allowance on all edges to wrong side. Baste to hold in position. Fold up other narrow end (not the one with inset panel) to form pocket of bag about 8 in. deep. Allowed 2 in. of main section to form base of bag, stitch side gussets in position, with right sides together and taking 1 in. turnings. Turn in seam allowance at top edge of gussets and baste. Cut main section and side gussets from lining material and stitch together in a similar way. Place lining in bag wrong sides together. Oversew neatly round top edge and all the way round flap section.

On each handle strip, press ½ in. seam allowances to wrong side. Place strips together, wrong sides facing, and machine stitch close to edges. From remainder of plastic-coated cotton fabric, cut 2 small strips, each about 1 in. by 2 in. Turn in raw edges and slipstitch, loop each small strip over one ring and stitch to side gusset of bag about 2 in. down from top edge. Take each end of handle through one ring, and stitch in place. Stitch press fastener to flap to fasten.

STITCH AND COLOUR KEY

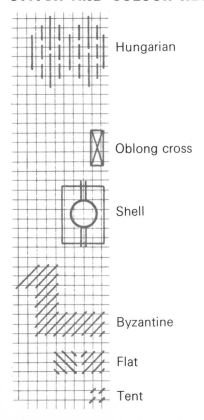

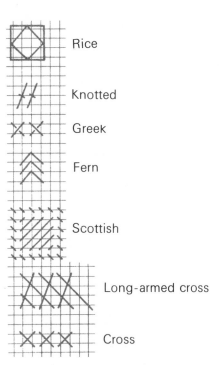

Hungarian

Oblong cross

Shell

Byzantine

Flat

Tent

Rice

Knotted

Greek

Fern

Scottish

Long-armed cross

Cross

All other stitches are variations of straight and slanting satin.

Note. Work areas marked 1 in black; areas marked 2 in white; areas marked 3 in black and white together.

traditional chair seat

Illustrated in colour on page 143.

MATERIALS

Of Coats Anchor Tapisserie Wool—16 skeins Black 0403, 2 skeins Cream 0386, 2 skeins Pale Pink 0894, 1 skein each of Carnation 023, Raspberry (medium) 069, Raspberry (dark) 071, Muscat Green 0281, Canary 0288, Forest Green (light) 0859, Forest Green (medium) 0861, Forest Green (dark) 0862, Mid Pink 0895, and Dark Pink 0896. $\frac{5}{8}$yd. double thread tapestry canvas, 27in. wide, 10 holes to 1in. A chair with an inset seat pad. Milward 'Gold Seal' tapestry needle No. 19. Upholstery tacks.

MEASUREMENTS

Finished seat measures approximately 16$\frac{1}{2}$in. at front edge, 13$\frac{3}{4}$in. at back edge, and 13$\frac{1}{2}$in. long.

DIAGRAM

Diagram A gives a little over a quarter of the pattern motif. Each background square on the diagram represents the double threads of the canvas

TO MAKE

Mark the centre of canvas both ways with a line of basting stitches then mark out total area of embroidery to fit seat pad. Prepare canvas, and mount it if you are using a frame. Work embroidery following diagram A and colour key. The blank arrows on the diagram mark the centre and should coincide with your basting stitches. Work other three quarters to correspond. Complete background in black.

TO COMPLETE

Stretch canvas, if necessary. Place the embroidery right side up centrally on the chair pad, fold back the unworked border of canvas and secure in position on the underside with tacks.

STITCH
Trammed tent

COLOUR KEY

- ⟋ Carnation
- ⠶ Pale Pink
- ⁒ Medium Forest Green
- ◣ Mid Pink
- ◤ Dark Pink
- ◆ Medium Raspberry
- ○ Light Forest Green
- ■ Dark Forest Green
- ▼ Muscat Green
- ◉ Canary
- ✕ Cream
- ☐ Black
- ● Dark Raspberry

DIAGRAM A

chatsworth
fender stool

MATERIALS
Of Coats Anchor Tapisserie Wool—48 skeins Mushroom 0981, 6 skeins Raspberry 0870, and 4 skeins Forest Green (dark) 0862. $\frac{5}{8}$yd. double thread tapestry canvas, 44in. wide, 10 holes to 1in. Stool with inset pad measuring approximately 14$\frac{1}{2}$in. by 38$\frac{1}{2}$in. Milward 'Gold Seal' tapestry needle No. 19. Upholstery tacks.

MEASUREMENTS
Finished seat measures approximately 14$\frac{1}{2}$in. by 38$\frac{1}{2}$in.

DIAGRAM
Diagram A gives a section of the complete design, showing how 3 fern motifs are linked together. Each background square on the diagram represents the double threads of the canvas.

TO MAKE
Mark the centre of canvas both ways with a line of basting stitches. Prepare canvas, and mount it, if you are using a frame. With the narrow end of canvas towards you, begin the embroidery centrally, following diagram A and the colour key. The blank arrows on the diagram mark the centre and should coincide with your basting stitches.

Work the section as given first, then continue to work on either side of this central group of motifs until there are 6 pink and 5 green ferns altogether. To complete embroidery, extend the background so that there are 30 rows of stitches from tips of ferns on each long side and 15 rows at each narrow end.

TO COMPLETE
Stretch the canvas, if necessary. Place the embroidery right side up centrally on the stool pad. Fold the unworked border of canvas back and secure in position on the underside with upholstery tacks.

STITCH
Trammed tent

COLOUR KEY

Mushroom
Raspberry
Forest Green

DIAGRAM A

book list

The following list represents a good general selection of books on the art of embroidery, published since the 19th century, which include chapters or sections devoted to needlepoint tapestry. The recently published titles should be readily available through most booksellers. The older books however may not be so easy to obtain, but are well worth trying to track down. Alternatively, the books can usually be consulted at most good reference libraries.

Mary Thomas's Dictionary of Embroidery Stitches
Hodder and Stoughton

Art of Embroidery
Schuette and Muller-Christensen
Thames and Hudson

Complete Book of Needlework
Ward Lock

Craft of Embroidery, A. Liley
Mills and Boon

Design in Embroidery, K. Whyte
Batsford-Branford

Canvas Embroidery for Beginners,
Sylvia Green
Studio Vista

Ideas for Canvas Work, Mary Rhodes
Batsford

Canvas Embroidery, Diana Springall
Batsford

Canvas Work
The Embroiderers Guild, London

**Embroidery Stitches
(USA Needlework Stitches),**
Barbara Snook
Batsford

The Stitches of Creative Embroidery,
Jacqueline Enthoven
Reinhold

Canvas Work and Design, Jennifer Gray
Batsford

Art in Needlework, Lewis F. Day
Batsford (1907)

Creative Needlework,
Solweig Hedin and Jo Springer
Fawcett Publications Inc.

Inspiration for Embroidery, C. Howard
Batsford

Ecclesiastical Embroidery, B. Dean
Batsford

Encyclopedia of Needlework,
Thérèse de Dillmont
D.M.C. Library, Mulhouse, France

Dictionary of Needlework,
S. F. A. Caulfeild and B. C. Saward
L. Upcott Gill, London (1903)

acknowledgements

Acknowledgements are due to the following people and organisations who generously loaned work or photographs from their collections, for inclusion as illustrations in this book:

Victoria and Albert Museum, London: cross stitch sample, page 5; Syon Cope, page 7; stumpwork panel, page 8; hangings on pages 10 and 16; cushion covers on pages 11 and 12; Bradford table carpet, page 13; Abraham and the Angels, page 14; purses on page 15; Spanish hangings on page 19; sampler on page 21; cross stitch sample, page 87.
City of Manchester Art Galleries: embroidered bag, page 24.
Contemporary Hangings (exhibition organiser: Mrs. Vera Sherman): Rhythm of Blue Verticals, by Myriam Gilby, page 26; Woven Hanging, by Tadek Beutlich, page 99.
Wm. Briggs and Co. Ltd.: Penelope designs illustrated on pages 6, 25, 54, 69, 70, 71, 78, 85, 95 and 102. These designs are available as complete needlework kits from store needlework departments and needlework shops.
Mrs. M. Craske, Hayes, Kent: tea cosy, page 37; sampler, page 44.
Barbara Snook: canvas work picture on page 35; various stitch samples.
Mrs. M. Bamber, Tatsfield, Kent: Berlin work tray, page 23; sampler, page 39.
Mrs. B. Relf, Knockholt, Kent: three kings picture, page 29; sampler, page 43; picture, page 63; cushion, page 66; design, page 94; sampler, page 97.
Mrs. D. Green, Orpington, Kent: kneeler design, page 88.
Mrs. M. Holden, West Wickham, Kent: stools on pages 65 and 68; traditional bag on page 67.
Marjorie Halligan: various designs and stitch samples throughout the book, also the following designs: sampler, page 53; cockerel hanging, page 72; owl picture, page 72; three cat cushion, page 89; beaded pincushion, page 141; square pincushion, page 149; cat pincushion, page 152; butterfly paperweight, page 154; rug wool and felt cushion, page 156; belt, page 158; Florentine spectacle case, page 160; inset panel bag, page 165.
J. & P. Coats Ltd., Glasgow: for all other designs in the chapter beginning on page 102.

index

USA EQUIVALENTS

In general, needle sizes in the USA are the same as those used in the United Kingdom. Canvas sizes and types are also similar. Thread qualities however vary slightly: in the USA, as a rule, threads are divided into fine mercerised, ordinary mercerised and heavy duty. Fine mercerised should be used with fine and sheer fabrics; ordinary with all medium-weight fabrics; heavy duty for thick and weighty fabrics and most furnishing fabrics. There are good-quality multi-purpose threads available both in the UK and the USA which can be used with all fabric types and weights.

If Clark's Anchor Stranded Cotton is not readily available, then J. & P. Coats Deluxe Six Strand Floss can be substituted, and will give satisfactory results. The colour range is wide, and there should be an equivalent shade for each shade of Anchor Stranded Cotton. If Coats Anchor Tapisserie Wool is not readily available, then any good-quality tapestry wool can be satisfactorily substituted.